The Christian Faith in Today's World

Michael Keene

Blackwell Education

FAMILY LIFE

1.1 What is a family?

What is a family? That's easy. My family is me, my sister and my Mum and Dad. Wait a minute, though – I forgot my Gran and Grandad. They're family too. And what about my other relations? Do they count?

Derek, 14

Derek was confused when he was asked to name the members of his family. You can begin to see why if you look at pictures **A** and **B**. The first thing you'll probably notice is that family **A** is much larger than family **B**. Not only are there more children, there are also three generations of people in the family group: children, parents and grandparents.

Extended and nuclear families

Family **A** includes aunts, uncles and cousins. This kind of family arrangement is called an **extended** family.

The much smaller family group in **B** is called a **nuclear** family. It is built around the 'nucleus' of parents and children.

---

1 You've probably met the term 'nucleus' in Biology. (If not, look it up in a dictionary.) Explain what a nucleus is, in your own words. Do you think this is a good way to describe a family like the one in **B**?
2 Draw up a table like the one below, listing the advantages and disadvantages of belonging to each type of family.

	Advantages	Disadvantages
Extended family		
Nuclear family		

Other forms of family life

Although the 'nuclear family' is the most popular arrangement for people in the UK, it is not the only

A *Three generations pose for the camera. Would you like to belong to an extended family like this?*

sort of family grouping. Surveys show that just 45% of people in this country live in a nuclear family. So what do the other 55% do? They may come into one of the following groups:

1 *The expanded family* Old people, the disabled or mentally handicapped people sometimes live together as a family and help to look after each other although they are not related to each other.
2 *The commune or community* Some people choose to live together and share work, child-care and property (more about this in Unit 1.2). Groups of religious people (eg monks or nuns) may live in a religious community.
3 *The reconstituted family* Divorced people who re-marry may bring children from their previous marriage. As a result, two families are brought together; children have a new step-parent and parents take on new step-children.
4 *The one-parent family* (more about this in Unit 1.3)

5 *The childless family* Some married couples choose not to have children; others find they are unable to have children. This group also includes older couples whose children have grown up and left home.

Then there are *single people*. About 25% of the adult UK population consists of single people: the unmarried, divorced or widowed. This group also includes people who are living together (cohabiting) but unmarried – legally they are considered to be single people.

---

3 Do any of the groups described above (1–5) not fit your idea of what makes a 'family'? Which one(s) and why?
4 Why do you think some married couples choose not to have children? Does the idea appeal to you? Why/why not? What do you think couples gain, or lose, by not having children?

Why is the family important?

Many people, including most Christians, feel that the family is very important. They point out that the family:

- gives the individual a sense of identity – this includes the person's social background, name, physical characteristics and mannerisms – and possibly also values and opinions;
- teaches the growing child how he or she is expected to behave (this is called 'socialisation') and something of the role he or she will play in society as an adult;
- provides the first close bond with other people. From the example of our parents and other family members we learn how to give and receive love; how to deal with our feelings; how to treat others with care and consideration; and how to share;
- is the best way of caring for the very young (and perhaps also the very old). Through the family, new life replaces those who have died.

Of course, all this applies only to the most perfect family. Very few families could live up to these ideals. Modern psychiatry shows that many problems and difficulties can be traced back to a person's background and early years.

---

5 What do you think of the list of important features about the family? Do you think it is true? idealistic? out-of-date? Discuss this in groups or hold a class debate.
6 Why is family life so important?

B *The nuclear family in modern Britain usually consists of mother, father and two children.*

What does the Bible say?

Mark 3.31–35
And his mother and his brothers came; and standing outside they sent to him and called him. And a crowd was sitting about him; and they said to him, 'Your mother and your brothers are outside, asking for you.' And he replied, 'Who are my mother and my brothers?'

And looking around on those who sat about him, he said, 'Here are my mother and my brothers! Whoever does the will of God is my brother, and sister, and mother.'

- Is Jesus rejecting his family? What point do you think he is trying to make?

A matter of opinion

Far from being the basis of a good society, the family, with its narrow privacy and tawdry secrets, is the source of all our discontents.

- What do you think the speaker meant?
- Do you agree? Give reasons for your answer.

1.2 Alternatives to the family

Sometimes my family really gets on my nerves. Either we argue all the time, or I feel smothered ... as if I'm not a person in my own right. There must be a better way ...

Anna, 16

Do you sometimes feel like Anna? Family life has its problems as well as its advantages. But is there a better way?

From time to time groups of people try to adopt an alternative way of living. A small group may decide to 'drop out' of conventional society, like the people in photograph **A**. Or the attempt may be on a much larger scale. This unit looks at two of the best-known experiments in communal living.

The Russian experiment

After the Russian Revolution in 1917, some of the revolutionaries attempted to abolish traditional family life. Experts in statistics calculated that Russians spent 36,000,000 hours a day doing household chores. They argued that this could be reduced to 6,000,000 hours if people lived in communes and shared out the tasks.

Collectives were set up to look after child-care, kitchen work, laundry services and so on, so that more women could take up full-time work. The marriage laws were reformed so that women gained equal rights with men. Divorce was made easier.

What happened?

The scheme soon ran into difficulties. The experts had not calculated just how much work was done

A *Some people reject the values and lifestyle of modern society and seek an 'alternative' way of life. How do you react to this picture? Do you think 'drop-outs' are irresponsible? Or do you find the idea attractive?*

by the family. The State collective nurseries could not meet the needs of all the children. Although making divorce easier was intended to benefit women, it actually meant that men simply walked out on their wives and children – who, in turn, needed still more State support.

The experiment was finally abandoned in 1934. Divorce became more difficult and the State began to emphasise the importance of marriage and family life again.

---

1 Why do you think the Russian experiment failed? Do you think the State can tell people how to live?

B *Workers on an Israeli kibbutz.*

The Israeli kibbutz

The modern state of Israel was founded in 1948. Soon after this a new system of communal living was introduced: the **kibbutz** (B). The idea was to raise the country's agricultural productivity by setting up communal farms (kibbutzim).

Kibbutz workers receive little or no payment. They share out the tasks: for example, some may harvest fruit, some work in the factory, some help in the kitchens and some look after the other workers' children.

Kibbutzim vary considerably in size and organisation. Workers have few personal possessions, but they receive board and lodging, health care, child care and education, and entertainment. Within the community, people do not need to go through any formal wedding ceremony, unless they want to. Instead, they may simply change their single room for a double one. When children are born, they are brought up by trained staff in a special Children's Home.

The future?

At no time since 1948 have more than 10% of Israel's population lived on a kibbutz. The present figure is around 4%. Many kibbutz workers are foreign volunteers who come for a few months or a year.

Kibbutzim still contribute a great deal to Israel's agricultural output, but the whole idea has come in for criticism. The generation of children born and brought up on the kibbutzim have argued that they want and need personal possessions, money and privacy.

---

2 Do you find the idea of life on a kibbutz attractive? What aspects of childhood and growing up do you think would be better on a kibbutz? What aspects might be worse?
3 Do you think there can be a successful alternative to family life?

What does the Bible say?

Romans 12.4–8
For as in one body we have many members (parts) and all the members do not have the same function, so we, though many, are one body in Christ, and individually members one of another. Having gifts that differ according to the grace given to us, let us use them; if prophecy, in proportion to our faith; if service, in our serving; he who teaches, in his teaching; he who exhorts, in his exhortation; he who contributes, in liberality; he who gives aid, with zeal; he who does acts of mercy, with cheerfulness.

- In what ways do these ideas match those behind a commune or kibbutz?
- How are they different?

A matter of opinion

The Russian Communist leader Lenin said:

The home life of a woman is a daily sacrifice to a thousand unimportant trivialities.

- What 'trivialities' do you think he meant?
- Do you agree?
- How have people attempted to solve this problem?

5

1.3 Single-parent families

My boyfriend, Darren, didn't want to know when I told him I was pregnant. And my friend said 'I suppose you'll have an abortion, then ... or will you have it adopted?' But I was determined to keep my baby. Jason's two now, and I wouldn't lose him for anything. Of course it's difficult being a one-parent family, but there are good times too ...

Janice, 18

Janice is one of over 1 million single-parent families in Britain today. The 'typical' family: two parents, two children, is perhaps not so typical after all. Over 5% of families in Britain are now headed by a single parent (**A**).

A Single-parent families: the facts

1 In 1971 there were 620,000 single-parent families in the UK. By 1976 this had increased to 750,000 and by 1980 it was 920,000. There are now over 1,000,000 single-parent families.

2 Over 1,600,000 children under the age of 16 are being brought up in single-parent families: 1,300,000 by their mother, 300,000 by their father.

3 In Britain, one family in eight is headed by a single parent.

---

1 If you were in Janice's situation, what would you have decided to do? Why?

Why are there so many single-parent families?

Before trying to answer this question, it's worth thinking about the different reasons why a single-parent family exists:

1 A girl or woman becomes pregnant accidentally but is unable or unwilling to marry the baby's father.

2 The husband or wife dies.

3 The husband or wife deserts their partner and leaves them with the children to bring up.

4 The parents divorce or separate and one (usually the mother) has custody of the children. The majority of single-parent families belong to this group.

5 More rarely, a woman elects to have a child and bring it up on her own – ie she does not intend to have a long-term relationship with the father.

The main factors to account for the number of single-parent families are the increase in the number of marriages that end in divorce or separation (see Unit 2.5); and the increase in illegitimate births (see Unit 2.8).

Problems for single parents

Single parents are likely to face many difficulties. Some receive help and support from families and friends – but many others have to cope with all the pressures and problems of raising a child on their own. There are practical problems, too:

- if they work full-time they have to find – and pay for – someone to look after the baby during working hours, as well as looking after the home and the child after work. All this leaves little or no time for rest or social life.
- if they do not work, they may have to rely on state benefits. A survey conducted in 1978 revealed that where the single parent did not work, 87% lived in poverty.

To help single-parent families cope with these difficulties, several organisations have been set up. The most famous is probably the Gingerbread Association for One-Parent families.

---

2 At the moment a man cannot be compelled to support his child unless he is married to, or divorced from, its mother. Do you think this is fair?

C   *There are now over 1,000,000 single-parent families in the UK.*

Effects on the child

Apart from possible financial/material difficulties, what is life like for the child, or children, in a single-parent family? Are there any advantages in growing up with only one parent? Look at **B**.

B

Drawbacks	Advantages
• miss everyday contact with one parent	• no longer have tensions arising from parents living together unhappily
• Mum or Dad may be lonely, tired or irritable	• the single parent can give undivided care and attention
• may experience prejudice from other children or adults	• forms an especially close bond with one parent

3 Can you add any drawbacks or advantages to the lists in **B**?

4 What problems do you think the family in **C** might face?

5 Why do you think most single-parent families are headed by the mother, rather than the father? Do you think a man would face greater difficulties in raising young children? Why?

A matter of opinion

My parents got divorced two years ago. Before that, they argued all the time. Life in our house was hell. Now my Mum and I can get on with our lives in peace. She gets tired after work, but I help her in the house. Some of my friends feel sorry for me – but I'm happier now than I've ever been.

Jackie, 15

• Do you think a child needs two parents? Why?
• Is one happy parent *really* better than two who argue?

MARRIAGE AND SEX
2.1 Friendship

What makes a good friend? **A** is how some 15-year-olds answered this question:

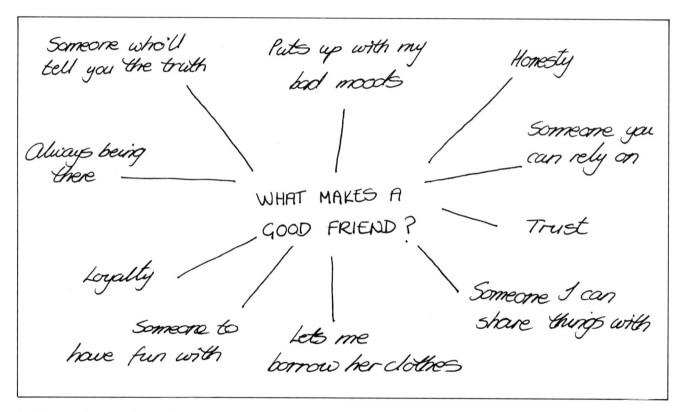

Someone who'll tell you the truth

Puts up with my bad moods

Honesty

Always being there

Someone you can rely on

WHAT MAKES A GOOD FRIEND?

Trust

Loyalty

Someone to have fun with

Lets me borrow her clothes

Someone I can share things with

A *What makes a good friend?*

A genuine friendship between two people is a serious thing. We usually expect friends to be all of the things mentioned above – and more.

Children begin to form friendships with others outside the family at a very early age (**B**). As they grow up, these relationships change. Some friendships break up or fade away. Others develop and become firm – sometimes lifelong – relationships.

---

1 What do you expect of your friends? What do they expect of you?

Where do we find our friends?

Of course, we can make friends with anyone. In practice, however, it is likely that most of our friends will:

- come from a background similar to our own;
- share at least some of our beliefs and opinions;
- live in our neighbourhood;
- have interests in common with us.

We build on these shared factors to form a lasting friendship. (Obviously, this doesn't mean that friends have to be *identical* – in a good friendship there is plenty of room for difference.)

B *Children make (and break) friendships very easily. But some childhood friendships last for life.*

What destroys a friendship?

You probably know what it's like when friends split up. Sometimes people move away or simply grow apart. But often the break-up is more sudden and painful. Perhaps the friends start competing with each other or there is a misunderstanding between them. Or maybe one friend is jealous of the other and envies his or her looks, possessions, abilities ... But how can we stop a friendship breaking up?

Sorting out disagreements

Arguments of one kind or another often broke out among the early Christians. Some groups disapproved of what others were doing, and there were wrangles over the proper way to behave. So they tried to find a procedure for sorting out these disputes. You can read about it in C.

C Matthew 18.15–17
'If your brother (Matthew did not necessarily mean a relation – the early Christians called each other 'brother' and 'sister') *sins against you, go and tell him his fault, between you and him alone. If he listens to you, you have gained your brother. But if he does not listen, take one or two others along with you, that every word may be confirmed by the evidence of two or three witnesses. If he refuses to listen to them, tell it to the church ...'*

The apostle Paul also had some advice about solving arguments (**D**).

D Ephesians 4.26
Do not let the sun go down on your anger.

---

2 Do you think the procedure described in **C** is a good way of solving disputes between friends? Why do you think Matthew suggests bringing in 'one or two others'? Can you think of any examples in everyday life where independent witnesses or arbitrators are brought in to settle disputes?
3 What do you think Paul meant in **D**? Do you think this is good advice?
4 What is a friend? Why are friends so important to us?

What does the Bible say?

Proverbs 7.17 *A friend loves at all times ...*

Proverbs 18.24 *A man of many companions may come to ruin; but there is a friend who sticks closer than a brother.*

Proverbs 27.6 *Wounds from a friend can be trusted ...*

John 15.13 *Greater love has no man than this; that he lay down his life for his friends.*

● Choose one of the statements above and explain what it means in your own words.

A matter of opinion

If I had to choose between betraying my friend and betraying my country, I hope I should have the guts to betray my country. (E M Forster)

● What do you think of this statement?
● Do you agree with it? Why?

2.2 Love

Love is never having to say you're sorry.
Love makes the world go round
Love is all you need.
Love is blind.

love *luv, n.* fondness: charity: an affection of the mind caused by that which delights: strong liking: devoted attachment to one of the opposite sex: sexual attachment: a love-affair: the object of affection: used as a term of endearment or affection: the god of love, Cupid, Eros: a kindness, a favour done (*Shak.*): the mere pleasure of playing, without stakes: in some games, no score. – *v.t.* to be fond of: to regard with affection: to delight in with exclusive affection: to regard with benevolence. – *v.i.* to have the feeling of love. – *adjs.* **lov'able, love'able** (*luv'e-bl*) worthy of love: amiable; **love'less**. – *n.* **love'lihead** (*rare*) love-liness. – *adv.* **love'lily** (*rare*). – *n.* **love'liness**. – *adj.* **love'ly** loving, amorous (*Shak.*): exciting admiration:

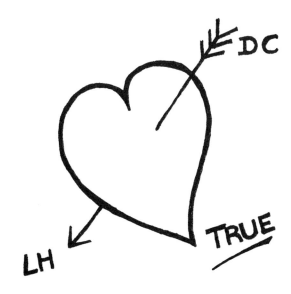

---

1 Which of these definitions of love do you think is nearest to the truth? Or can you think of another one?

We all use the word 'love' a lot. But we use it to describe a whole range of very different emotions. We may say we 'love' peanut butter or a famous pop star; we love our parents, brothers and sisters; we may be 'in love' with our boyfriend or girl-friend.

Love at first sight?

Is it possible to love someone you've never met (like a pop star) – or someone you've just met for the first time? Probably not – but it *is* possible to experience very strong feelings about that person – which is perhaps what we mean when we talk of 'falling in love'. Sometimes people also call this 'infatuation'.

When we fall in love with someone our feelings can be almost overwhelming. Physical feelings are especially strong. We want to be close to that person all the time. Sometimes the relationship doesn't really develop any further than this. But sometimes the emotional bond deepens and grows. Physical feelings are still important, but along with them are tenderness, affection, responsibility and commitment to the other person – really 'loving' them, as well as being 'in love'.

---

2 In your own words, explain the differences between infatuation, being 'in love with' someone, and loving someone.

What does the Bible say?

If you look at a copy of the New Testament you'll see that the word 'love' appears quite frequently. In the original Greek, however, there are *four* words – used to describe different kinds of love:

1 *Eros* – this is love based simply on physical attraction (it gives us our word 'erotic').
2 *Philia* – this is the sort of love that exists between friends.
3 *Storge* – this is the love we have for members of our family.
4 *Agape* – this is Christian love. This is different from the other forms of love because it includes

loving people to whom we feel no attraction; people who do not respond to us; even people we don't like.

Christian love, therefore, demands a great deal of people. Most of us find it fairly easy to love people who love us – but in Matthew's gospel Jesus expects his followers to do more than this (**A**):

A Matthew 5.43, 44
You have heard that it was said: 'Love your neighbour and hate your enemy'. But I say to you: love your enemies and pray for those who persecute you.'

---

3 Have you recently had a disagreement with someone? If so, try to remember what happened.
   a) How did you react?
   b) How did the conflict end?
   c) Would you have found it difficult to 'love your enemy' in that situation? Why?
   d) What do you think would have happened if you had tried to follow Jesus' instructions?

4 Who do you think Jesus meant by 'your enemies'?
5 Can people be 'commanded' to love? Why/why not?
6 What is distinctive about Christian love?

What does the Bible say?

The following passage comes from the New Testament letter to the Corinthians. It is sometimes called the 'hymn of love':

1 Corinthians 13.4–7
Love is patient and kind; love is not jealous or boastful; it is not arrogant or rude. Love does not insist on its own way; it is not irritable or resentful; it does not rejoice at wrong, but rejoices in the right. Love bears all things, believes all things, hopes all things, endures all things.

- To which sort of love do you think the writer was referring?
- *Either:* rewrite this passage in your own words; *or:* compose your own hymn of love.

2.3 Sex

I should say that me and my mates spend about 50% of our time talking about sex! You know, making jokes, discussing what we've seen on telly, what girls we fancy ... Of course, we all exaggerate a bit – I mean, no-one's going to admit they don't know all about it, are they?

Andy, 16

Ask any young person what worries them most and sex is likely to be near the top of the list. Why is sex still such a 'taboo' subject? Why are so many people – like Andy – embarrassed when talking about sex?

Sex and life

Sex is a normal human activity which plays an important part in most people's lives. We are all sexual beings. Even very young children experience sexual feelings.

For most young children, of course, sex is not a problem. (The exceptions are those children who sadly become victims of child abuse – see Unit 9.4.) Questions about sex arise when we reach puberty – usually in our early teens. Puberty marks the physical change from child to adult. Along with this physical development come changes to our emotions and interests – the girl who, not so long ago, was playing with dolls, is now more interested in make-up. The boy who went fishing goes to discos instead.

Puberty is a time of confusion and questions – many of them about sex. Although our bodies are reaching sexual maturity, very few people are ready for a full-scale sexual relationship at the age of 13 or 14. That is one reason why it is illegal for young people in Britain under 16 to have sexual intercourse.

A

Chat up lines for girls

SEX SHOP MADNESS

two timing without getting caught

How to meet gorgeous girls...

What turns men on?

DATING the truth revealed

1 How do you react to advertisements and articles like the ones in **A**? Do you find them offensive? boring? a harmless bit of fun? Explain why.

What is sex for?

The answer, simply, is: reproduction. Sexual intercourse or mating is the 'mechanics' by which a species (in this case, humankind) is kept alive. This message is reinforced in the Biblical story of creation, in which God says to Adam and Eve:

'*Be fruitful and increase in number, fill the earth . . .*'

Only for human beings, it seems, is sex a pleasurable activity in its own right.

We are surrounded by 'messages' about sex in the media, on TV, in films (see **A**). No wonder many young people are confused. On the one hand, sex is treated lightly – have fun, enjoy yourself, don't think about the consequences! On the other, it is seen as something wicked and shameful – something that 'nice' people don't do at all! The former, casual attitude leads to promiscuous behaviour. The latter approach may mean that a person is afraid of any form of contact or love.

For most people, sex is special. It is a physical expression of their love for and commitment to each other. As such, a sexual relationship is something to be enjoyed – but with a sense of responsibility towards each other and towards society. For most Christians, this sort of relationship will take place within marriage (see Unit 2.4).

2 Over the next week, make a collection of magazine or newspaper articles which seem to give a 'message' about sex, and write down what you think that message is. For example:

Hairspray ad.

Using this will make women irresistible

3 What problems or dangers could result from a promiscuous attitude towards sex? (Look at Units 2.8 and 2.10 to help you)?
4 State three reasons why you think a responsible attitude to sex is important.
5 Most Christians believe that sex outside marriage is wrong. Do you agree?

Life without sex

Most people have sexual feelings. But some choose not to enter into a sexual relationship – either for a period or for their whole lives.

● A *virgin* is someone who has never had sexual intercourse. In the past it was expected that a woman should be a virgin when she married and she might even have to prove it. Interestingly, this was not required of men. Today many couples live together before they marry (see Unit 2.4) or will have had other sexual partners. Some people, however, wish to 'save' themselves for the very special marriage relationship.

● A person who is *celibate* does not have a sexual relationship. A person may choose to spend a period without sex. Some people take a vow of celibacy (usually for religious reasons) which means that they will never have sex. Roman Catholic priests are required to be celibate.

6 Why do you think a person might choose a life without sex? What problems do you think he or she would face?

A matter of opinion

A girl plays at sex for which she is not ready, because fundamentally what she wants is love; and the boy plays at love, for which he is not ready, because what he wants is sex.

Mary Calderone

● Do you think men and women look at sex and love differently? If so, how?

MARRIAGE AND SEX
2.4 Marriage – the facts

I expect I'll get married – but not for at least ten years. I want to have some fun and see the world before I settle down with a wife and kids. I'd probably live with the girl first, to make sure it would all work out. As for the wedding, I'd just want a quick Registry Office do – I couldn't stand all the fuss of a church wedding.

Mark, 18

Mark is fairly typical of his generation. People are waiting longer to marry now than they did 20 years ago, and over 50% of couples live together before they marry.

Look at **A**. You can see from the chart that the number of marriages per year in Britain has gone down since 1971. But there is no sign that *marriage* itself is dying out. Over 90% of women and 80% of men are married before they reach the age of 30.

	Marriages (thousands)			
	1971	1976	1981	1986
First marriages	369	282	263	254
Total marriages	459	406	398	394

A *Marriages in Britain 1971–1986.*

---

1 Why do you think people wait longer before they get married? At what age would you like to get married? Why?

2 Look at **A**. Why do you think fewer people are getting married now than in 1971?

Why marry?

People get married for all sorts of complicated reasons. Some of the most common are:

- to express their love and commitment to one another
- so that they can live together with the approval of family, friends and society in general
- to gain the security of a permanent relationship
- so that they can have children and bring them up in a stable environment
- to get away from home and 'prove' that they are adult
- so that their sexual drives can be channelled
- for friendship and companionship

---

3 Do you think that these are all good reasons for getting married? Which do you think are the three most important? Can you think of any others?

Church or registry office?

People in the United Kingdom can marry either in a religious building (church, temple, mosque, synagogue etc) which is licensed for marriages, or in a Registry Office. Today, more people opt for a civil (Registry Office) ceremony.

---

4 Carry out a survey of your class to find out how many people would like a religious wedding ceremony and how many would prefer a Registry Office wedding.

The Church Service

A wedding in a Christian church combines legal and religious elements. The legal parts confirm that

B *Why do you think fewer people now opt for a traditional church wedding?*

the couple are 'officially' married – in the eyes of the law and of society. The religious elements sum up the Christian view of marriage:

1 The couple are told that God's purposes for marriage are:
   - for them to live together and support each other;
   - for them to enjoy sex with each other;
   - for them to have children.
2 The priest or minister asks questions to make sure that there is no legal reason why the marriage cannot go ahead, and that the bride and groom really wish to marry.
3 The bride's father (or another relative) 'gives' her to the groom.
4 The groom gives the bride a ring (or the couple exchange rings) as a symbolic 'seal' on their love.
5 The priest or minister declares that the couple are married *in the sight of God*.
6 The priest or minister then asks for God's blessing on the couple's married life together.

7 The couple sign a certificate in front of two witnesses.

---

5 From the list above, choose two examples of religious elements in the Christian wedding ceremony, and two examples of 'legal' elements.
6 What does the procedure tell you about the Christian view of marriage?
7 Some people think that it is wrong for a couple who are not Christians to be married in church. What do you think?

C is an extract from the Church of England wedding service; **D** comes from a Registry Office ceremony.

C *I take thee to be my wedded husband (wife), to have and to hold, from this day forward, for better and worse, for richer and poorer, in sickness and in health, to love and to cherish, till death us do part, according to God's holy law, and thereto I give you my troth (promise).*

D *Before you are joined together in matrimony, it is my duty to warn you of the solemn and binding character of the vows you are about to make. Marriage, according to the laws of this country, is the union of one man with one woman, voluntarily entered into, to the exclusion of all others.*

---

8 List the main differences between **C** and **D**. In what ways do they give a similar view of marriage?
9 Do you think that marriage is relevant to today's world?

Sex and marriage

Surveys show that only about 20% of the population are now virgins when they marry. About 50% of the population have lost their virginity before they reach their 18th birthday. Statistics like these alarm many Christians. They point out the personal and social consequences of sexual activity outside marriage. In particular, they draw attention to:

- the number of marriages which break down because one of the partners has been unfaithful;
- the risk of unwanted pregnancy – and linked to this, the increasing number of abortions and of one-parent families;

- the danger of sexually-transmitted diseases and AIDS (see Unit 2.9)

Most Christians condemn 'casual' sex, but some are prepared to accept that a couple may have a committed relationship outside marriage. For others, however, any sexual relationship outside marriage is 'living in sin'.

When a marriage fails...

What does the future hold for the couple in photograph B? Will they still be together in 10 years time? Or in 20?

When they get married, most people hope that their marriage will last for life. Christians believe that marriage is a life-long commitment. Catholics, in particular, argue that marriage vows cannot be broken.

Sadly, however, many marriages fail. An estimated one in three marriages ends in divorce. The next two units look at some of the controversial issues surrounding divorce.

Not every broken marriage ends in divorce. What are the alternatives?

1 *Separation* – a couple live apart, but remain married. (This may be for the two or five-year period before their divorce is granted.) It is illegal for either partner to re-marry. The Roman Catholic Church does not recognise divorce (see Unit 2.4); Catholics whose marriage fails live in separation.
2 *Desertion* – a husband or wife simply walks out and does not return.
3 *An 'empty' marriage* – the couple continue to live together even though they no longer love each other, or may even dislike each other. Many couples stay together for financial reasons, or for the sake of the children.

---

10 Do you think any of these alternatives is preferable to divorce? Why?

What does the Bible say?

The Christian view of marriage is based in part on the teachings of the Old Testament. The ancient Hebrews believed that every girl had to be a virgin at the time of her marriage and remain completely faithful to her husband afterwards.

Proverbs 31.10–31
A good wife ... is far more precious than jewels. The heart of her husband trusts in her ... She does him good, and not harm, all the days of her life. She seeks wool and flax, and works with willing hands ... She rises while it is yet night and provides food for her household...

Of course, every man wanted to marry the 'ideal' woman! In marriage, the two of them would then become like one person. This view of marriage is laid down in the creation story:

Genesis 2.24
For this reason a man will leave his father and mother and be united to his wife, and they will become one flesh.

When he was questioned about the legality of divorce, Jesus reminded his questioners of this view of marriage

Matthew 19. 4–6
And Pharisees came up to him and tested him by asking, 'Is it lawful to divorce one's wife for any cause?' He answered, 'Have you not read that he who made them from the beginning made them male and female, and said, "For this reason a man shall leave his father and mother and be joined to his wife, and the two shall become one." So they are no longer two but one. What therefore God has joined together, let no man put asunder.'

In their married life, the husband and wife had different roles – each was to complement (complete) the other:

Genesis 2.18
The Lord God said, 'It is not good for man to be alone. I will make him a helper fit for him.'

- What do you think about this view of marriage?
- Look back at the section on Christian marriage. In what ways is the wedding service based on the Bible?

A matter of opinion

The Church of England Book of Common Prayer begins the Wedding Service with the words:

Dearly beloved, we are gathered together in the sight of God, and in the face of this congregation, to join together this man and this woman in holy matrimony.

- What does this tell you about the Christian view of marriage?

2.5 Divorce – the facts

My brother and I often heard our parents arguing, but we had no idea that they were going to split up. When they said they were getting a divorce, it felt like the end of the world. I can remember thinking it was my fault, somehow. It took us a long time to get over the shock. Even now, I sometimes dream that they could get back together again ...

Jenny, 14

Jenny's experience is a very common one today. One in three marriages in Great Britain ends in divorce.

Many people think that it is too easy for couples to get a divorce. But this wasn't always the case. Before 1857, divorce was a lengthy, long drawn out and very expensive legal process. **A** is by the Victorian novelist, Charles Dickens:

A *Why, you'd have to go to the Doctors' Commons with a suit* (a legal petition), *and you'd have to go to the House of Lords with a suit, and it would cost you (if it was a case of plain sailing) I suppose from £1000 to £1500, or even twice that money.*

Charles Dickens, *Hard Times*

(£1000 was a small fortune in Victorian England. Only the very rich would therefore be able to obtain a divorce.)

Changes in the law

In 1857 Parliament passed the Matrimonial Causes Act. This made divorce procedure easier and less expensive. Both men and women could apply for a divorce, although it was much easier for men:

- a woman had to demonstrate that her husband had committed adultery and also some other matrimonial offence, such as desertion or cruelty;
- a man simply had to prove that his wife had committed adultery.

Although divorce was now much easier, it was still beyond the means of ordinary people. Moreover, a great deal of stigma was attached to divorce. A

person (especially a woman) caught up in a divorce case would be rejected by 'polite' society.

---

1 Do you think the 1857 Act was fair to women? What does this suggest about Victorian attitudes?

In 1923 another Matrimonial Causes Act put men and women on the same footing. Now a husband or a wife could obtain a divorce on the grounds of adultery alone.

Legislation in 1937 extended the *grounds* (reasons or causes) for divorce, to include desertion, cruelty and insanity as well as adultery. The number of divorces continued to rise (see **B**).

During the Second World War and the years

B *Divorces in Britain 1905–1986.*

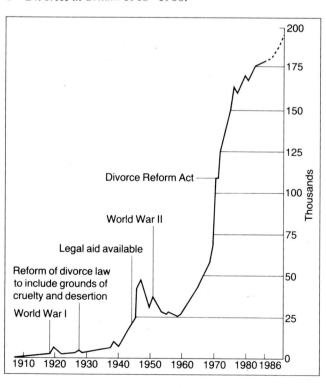

which followed, many marriages broke up. But divorce was still very expensive – many couples simply couldn't afford it. At the end of the 1940s the Legal Aid scheme (which helps people who are unable to pay legal fees) was extended to cover divorce.

The Divorce Reform Act

Parliament passed the Divorce Reform Act in 1969 and it became law on 1 January 1971. This law made major changes in divorce procedure. People could now obtain a divorce if they could show that their marriage had *irretrievably broken down* (ie that there was no chance of them getting back together again). In order to prove that a marriage has failed, the husband or wife could claim that:

- their partner had committed adultery.
- their partner had shown mental or physical cruelty
- their partner had deserted them

If both partners agree to get a divorce, it is granted after they have lived apart for two years (technically considered 'desertion'). If only one person wants the divorce, a five-year separation is necessary. The divorcing couple have to complete a simple legal procedure; they do not normally need to appear in court. Around 180,000 divorces now take place in Great Britain each year.

Some people feel that the divorce laws should be stricter. They argue that divorce is now so easy that:

- couples no longer see marriage as a long-term commitment;
- couples are not prepared to work at their marriage – as soon as difficulties arise, they opt for divorce;
- divorce devalues the whole institution of marriage.

---

2 Do you think divorce is now 'too easy'?

Who wins?

Divorce may now be much easier – but it is still a painful and difficult experience for all involved. Couples may experience a great sense of failure at the break-up of their marriage. One or both partners may suddenly be left to face life alone. There

C

may be bitter arguments over money and property (see C). And, of course, there are the children:

- there are about a million single-parent families in Great Britain. A high proportion of these result from divorce or failed marriages.
- 75% of all divorcing couples have children – 75% of these under the age of 16. There are thus about 1,250,000 children under the age of 16 who have been affected by their parents' divorce.

A matter of opinion

Divorce may be common, but that doesn't make it any easier. As well as the pain of the break-up, you're left with a terrible sense of guilt. Was it my fault? Could we have made a go of it? Having to make a new life on your own, after years of being part of a couple, is terrifying.

- Do you think people enter into marriage – and divorce – too lightly? Why/why not?

By way of definition

- *divorce* – the legal termination of a marriage
- *adultery* – for a married person to have sexual intercourse with someone other than their husband or wife
- *Legal Aid* – a grant which helps people to pay their legal costs

2.6 Christians divided about divorce

My cousin was divorced five years ago. Then last year she met Brian (he's divorced too) and they decided to get married. She wanted a church service, but the local vicar refused to do it – he said they'd have to go to the Registry Office. Yet when they went to Brian's vicar he agreed straight away and didn't make any fuss at all. I don't understand it . . .

Anneka, 15

Christians all over the world are divided on the question of divorce. Many maintain that marriage is an unbreakable agreement between two people, made in the presence of God. Others argue that a broken marriage is better ended in the interests of all concerned; in an ideal world there would be no need for divorce, but this world is far from ideal and divorce is an unpleasant part of life. Some adopt a middle line, saying that divorce is permissible only on grounds of adultery or desertion.

In Britain:

- the Roman Catholic Church will not accept divorce. However, some marriages can be 'annulled' or declared 'null and void' as if they had never happened. This releases the couple to marry again. Grounds for such a declaration might be if one of the couple had insisted on using a contraceptive, which is against the ruling of the Catholic Church (see Unit 2.6).
- the Church of England accepts divorced people, but will not usually re-marry them. In some circumstances, however, a vicar may agree to marry a divorced person and can obtain special permission from his Bishop.
- most Protestant Free Churches (such as the Baptists, Methodists, United Reformed Church . . .) will allow divorced people to marry in church, but the minister has the right to refuse if he or she disagrees with this.

---

1 Do you think divorced people should be allowed to marry in church? Why?

The background

Jewish law

According to an old Jewish law a man could divorce his wife if he found 'some indecency' in her (**A**).

A *If a man marries a woman who becomes displeasing to him because he finds something indecent about her; and he writes her a certificate of divorce, gives it to her and sends her from his house . . .*

However, there was much debate about what the 'indecency' might be. At the time of Jesus, three important Jewish rabbis (teachers) argued about this point:

- one maintained that the 'indecency' must be adultery by the wife;
- the second argued that it could cover her failure to run the home properly;
- and a third taught that a man could divorce his wife simply because he was not 'happy' with her.

Jewish law did not allow a wife to divorce her husband.

What did Jesus say about divorce?

Some of the Pharisees, or Jewish leaders, asked Jesus a trick question about divorce:

Matthew 19.3–9
He answered, 'Have you not read that he who made them from the beginning made them male and female, and said, "For this reason a man shall leave his father and mother and be joined to his wife, and the two shall become one?" So they are no longer two but one. What therefore God has joined together, let no man put asunder.'
    They said to him, 'Why then did Moses command one to give a certificate of divorce, and to put her away?'

He said to them, 'For your hardness of heart Moses allowed you to divorce your wives, but from the beginning it was not so. And I say to you: whoever divorces his wife, except for unchastity, and marries another, commits adultery.'

Jesus reminded his listeners about the purpose of marriage and the sort of relationship God had intended it to be. Moses, the great Jewish law-giver, had allowed divorce, because people failed to live up to this ideal. In Mark's Gospel, Jesus goes on:

Mark 10.11–12
'Whoever divorces his wife and marries another, commits adultery against her; and if she divorces her husband and marries another, she commits adultery.'

In Matthew, however, Jesus admits one reason for divorce:

'Whoever divorces his wife, except for unchastity, and marries another, commits adultery.'

Saint Paul was even more stern in his condemnation of divorce, although he seemed to accept the necessity for separation.

I Corinthians 7.10.11.27
... the wife should not separate from her husband (but if she does, let her remain single or else be reconciled to her husband) – and ... the husband should not divorce his wife.

... if any brother has a wife who is an unbeliever, and she consents to live with him, he should not divorce her. If any woman has a husband who is an unbeliever ... she should not divorce him.

- Under what circumstances did Jesus permit divorce?
- What is your opinion of divorce?

A matter of opinion

One Church of England vicar writes:

To those who have no connection with the Church and want marriage after divorce, I am afraid I offer nothing apart from an apology, and an explanation that the Church is trying to proclaim the importance of faithfulness in marriage, however hard that may sound. But to those who are genuine members of the Church, I always offer some kind of service after a Civil Ceremony in the Registry Office ... It is certainly important for genuine Christians to receive the blessing of God and his support as they commit themselves in this way, and for that to be given by the Church to which they belong ...

- Do you think this is an acceptable compromise?

2.7 Contraception

Dear Maj,

I don't know what to do. I think I might be pregnant ..... He said it would be alright – you never get caught the first time. But was he right?

What shall I do? I daren't tell my parents, and I can't go to the doctor because he's a family friend .....

You've probably seen desperate letters like **A** in magazine 'problem pages'. How would you reply?

Despite the emphasis on sex in the media and sex education in schools, many young people – like Debbie and her boyfriend – remain surprisingly ignorant about sex and contraception. It's tempting to think 'It couldn't happen to me' – but it is worth remembering that each time a couple makes love, around 300,000,000 sperms are released into the woman's body. It takes just one of these sperms to fertilise the egg. To avoid unwanted pregnancy, therefore, effective contraception is essential.

Forms of contraception

Any person – male or female – entering a sexual relationship needs to be well-informed about the methods of contraception available, and to decide which is right for him or her. **B** lists the main forms of contraception available.

---

1 There was a public outcry when the pill first became available in the 1960s. Many people feared it would lead to irresponsible sex and promiscuity. Were they right?

2 Do you think more could be done to inform young people about contraception? If so, what?

The 'Gillick case'

If Debbie goes to her doctor he or she will advise her on contraception and may prescribe the pill. Do you think the doctor should tell Debbie's parents, since she is under-age?

In 1985 Mrs Victoria Gillick, a mother of 10, argued that girls under 16 should not be given contraceptive advice or treatment without the consent of their parents. She went to court over this issue and there was a lengthy legal battle. The first judgement was in Mrs Gillick's favour. Finally, however, the House of Lords decided that girls under the age of 16 had the legal capacity to consent to medical treatment – including contraception – providing that the girl in question could give 'informed consent' (that is, was able to understand the implications of what she was doing).

---

3 Do you think the House of Lords' verdict was the right one? Why?

B

Female

The Pill – over 3,000,000 women in Britain take a contraceptive pill every day. 50,000,000 women worldwide use this form of contraception. It is claimed to be about 98% reliable, but some women suffer side-effects.

The IUD or coil – a plastic or metal device placed in the uterus by a doctor and left there.

The cap or diaphragm – a circular, rubber device which the woman fits over the neck of her cervix before she makes love.

Sterilisation – an operation to cut the Fallopian tubes along which the egg travels each month. Sterilisation makes a woman permanently infertile.

Male

The condom or sheath – a tube of thin latex which is fitted over the penis to catch the sperm. It also offers some protection against AIDS and other venereal disease.

Vasectomy (male sterilisation) – an operation to cut the two tubes which carry the sperm.

Two other forms of contraception offer only poor protection:
Rhythm method – some couples prefer not to use any 'artificial' form of contraception, often for religious reasons. The rhythm method relies on an accurate record of the woman's monthly cycle, to work out the most fertile times. The couple avoid making love at this time ...

Withdrawal – the man withdraws his penis from the woman before ejaculation (releasing sperm). Highly unreliable!

Christians and birth control

In the early part of this century contraception was a very controversial issue. Most churches were strongly opposed to the idea of 'birth prevention'. Gradually, most churches realised that birth control was a great benefit to many women and families.

The Roman Catholic Church, however, has maintained its stand against all artificial forms of contraception. In 1968 Pope Paul VI issued a declaration called the *Humanae Vitae* (**C**). In it, he laid down two principles about sexual intercourse:

1 It should strengthen the bond that already exists between a husband and wife.
2 It should always be open to the possibility of new life (ie pregnancy).

C *Humanae Vitae 25 July 1968*
... condemned is any action, which either before, or at the moment of, or after sexual intercourse is specifically intended to prevent procreation – whether as an end or as a means ... It is never lawful, even for the gravest reasons, to do evil that good may come of it ...

The Pope concluded that all forms of artificial birth control would break these principles and must therefore be forbidden to Catholics. The only permissible form of contraception is 'natural family planning' or the rhythm method, which is highly unreliable.

Some people argue that in this statement the Pope was condemning thousands of women to poverty, exhaustion – possibly even death – caused by having too many children.

Others maintain that the world's population is increasing far too rapidly – especially in poorer countries; they feel that the Catholic teaching is wrong and irresponsible. You can read more about the 'population explosion' in Unit 10.3

---

3 Would you agree with many Roman Catholics that contraception is 'unnatural' and against the will of God? If not, how would you answer this argument?

What does the Bible have to say?

Genesis 1.22 *God blessed them and said: 'Be fruitful and increase in number ...*
Psalm 127 4,5
Like arrows in the hand of a warrior are sons born in one's youth.
Blessed is the man whose quiver is full of them.

● Do you think children are a blessing? Why?

2.8 Homosexuality

I can't remember when I first realised that I might be gay ... 'Coming out' was the most difficult thing, especially telling my parents. They were very good about it, but they didn't really understand – how could they? It's taken them a long time to accept it and begin to treat me like a normal human being.

Tom, 19

Tom is part of a large minority group in Britain: **homosexuals**. Around 10% of the population are homosexual, or have a strong sexual preference for members of their own sex.

Why are some people homosexual?

Many theories have been suggested to explain why people are – or become – homosexual.

1 Some experts think that people are born homosexual; it is part of their genetic make-up and they can do nothing about it.
2 Some people argue that family background or social circumstances affect a person's sexual development. Psychiatrists suggest that boys who have an unnaturally strong link with their mothers, and weak or difficult relationships with

their fathers, are more likely to develop homosexual preferences.

3 Another theory is that all of us have the potential to be either homosexual or heterosexual. How we turn out depends on influences in childhood and our early sexual experiences.

Homosexuality and the law

If Tom had been around 30 years ago, he would have found life much more difficult. Until 1967 it was against the law to be a practising homosexual. If detected, homosexuals faced heavy fines and/or imprisonment. Some became the victims of unscrupulous blackmailers.

In 1967 the Government passed new legislation covering England and Wales. This made it legal to have a homosexual relationship, as long as it is:

- between consenting adults over the age of 21;
- conducted in private.

This does not apply to Scotland, or to members of the Merchant Navy or the armed forces, where it is still illegal to be a practising homosexual.

Most countries in Europe now permit homosexual relationships, although the age of consent varies. In Hungary, for example, it is 10, whereas in Spain it is 23.

---

1 Do you think the relaxation in laws governing homosexuality was a good thing? Give your reasons.

Christians and homosexuality

Homosexuality has been the subject of much debate among Christians. There are, of course, many Christians who are themselves homosexual or lesbian.

Some Christians condemn homosexuals as unnatural or sinful. They base this attitude on Bible passages like the following:

A Leviticus 18.22
Do not lie with a man as one lies with a woman. That is detestable.

B I Corinthians 6.9
Neither the immoral nor idolaters nor adulterers nor homosexuals ... will inherit the Kingdom of God.

(As far as we know, Jesus said nothing about homosexuality.)

But by no means all Christians are so harsh in their approach. In 1987 the General Synod of the Church of England (the Church of England's governing body) held a debate on what the church's attitude towards homosexuality should be. It decided that no-one should be criticised for having homosexual *feelings* – but that homosexual *acts* are unchristian.

The Methodist church is even more tolerant. C comes from a report issued in 1979:

C *For homosexual men and women permanent relationships characterised by love can be appropriate and the Christian way of expressing their sexuality.*

---

2 Is it realistic to accept that a person may have strong feelings for a member of their own sex, but then expect them to do nothing about it?
3 According to **A**, what characteristic should mark a Christian homosexual relationship?
4 Photograph **D** shows a homosexual couple who have just been married. How do you react to the photograph? Can you explain your reaction?

By way of definition

- *heterosexual* – person who feels sexually attracted towards the opposite sex.
- *homosexual* – someone sexually attracted to the same sex
- *lesbian* – a female homosexual

A matter of opinion

As a Christian, I believe that I should fight against injustice and inequality. That involves campaigning for the rights of homosexuals and trying to overcome blind prejudice.

- Do you agree or disagree with this viewpoint? Explain you reasons.

D *Do you find this photograph shocking? Funny? Discuss your response with a friend. Try to work out why you reacted in that way.*

2.9 Aids

A

Tragic aids victim says 'I'll sue the NHS'

Aids total set to double in years

AIDS ALERT!

'It's a judgement' says vicar

New AIDS risk in . . .

During the 1980s a new and terrifying disease hit the headlines: AIDS or Acquired Immune Deficiency Syndrome (**A**). Is this the plague of the 20th century, or a punishment sent by God for human wickedness, as some maintain? In 1987 the British Government produced a leaflet which was distributed to every household in Britain (**B**). **C** is an extract from the leaflet.

C *Any man or woman can get the AIDS virus depending on their behaviour. It is not just a homosexual disease. There is no cure and it kills.*
By the time you read this probably 300 people will have died in this country. It is believed that a further 30,000 carry the virus. The number is rising and will continue to rise unless we all take precautions.

---

1 How do you react to this warning? Does it make you feel concerned? alarmed? bored?
2 Can a warning like this prompt people to change, or is it more likely to cause panic? Why?
3 Conduct a survey in your class to find out how much people know about AIDS. Do you think the Government campaign was effective?

What is AIDS?

AIDS is caused by a virus – the Human Immunodeficiency Virus (HIV). If the virus enters the bloodstream, it attacks the cells which maintain the body's natural defence mechanisms. Inside a cell, the virus multiplies until eventually it destroys the cell. The person's defence system begins to fail, and he or she is unable to recover from infections.

There is no cure for AIDS. Death is slow and drawn out. Victims succumb to a variety of illnesses and infections. However, not everyone who contracts the HIV virus goes on to develop AIDS, although as yet scientists do not know why.

Who catches AIDS – and how?

As the AIDS panic spread, so did rumours about how it could be caught. In fact, it is NOT easy to catch the HIV virus. Unlike other viruses, such as colds, or flu, HIV cannot be carried in the air, consumed in food, or picked up from any everyday

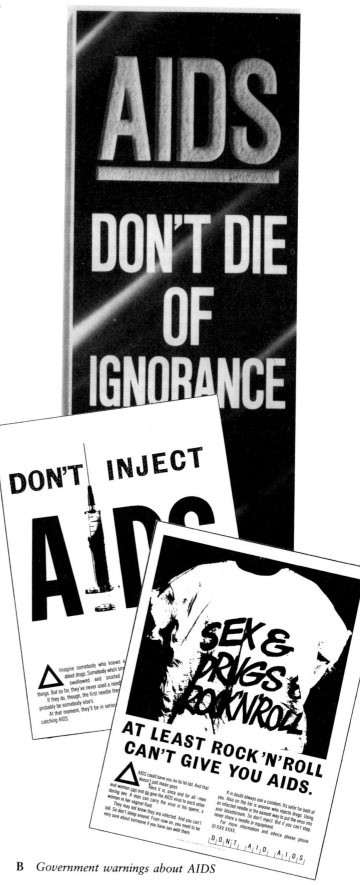

B *Government warnings about AIDS*

24

activity such as sharing cups, shaking hands, using a swimming pool or public toilet, or kissing.

HIV is transmitted in only three ways:

1 Through contaminated blood. Until recently there was a risk that supplies of blood used for transfusions might be contaminated by HIV. Haemophiliacs, who need regular blood transfusions, were especially in danger. Very sadly, some contracted the virus before the risk was recognised. Now, in the UK, all blood is carefully screened – but this is not the case in some other countries.
2 Through using a contaminated needle to inject yourself. Drug users who share needles or syringes risk acquiring the virus.
3 Through sexual intercourse (especially anal sex). HIV is transmitted through semen and vaginal fluid.

Who is at risk?

Because of the ways in which AIDS is transmitted, certain groups of the population are particularly at risk. They are:

- homosexual men
- drug users who share needles
- sexual partners of those who are infected
- anyone who has a large number of sexual partners
- babies of mothers who have AIDS, since the virus can be transmitted through a mother's milk

The new lepers

Much of the panic about AIDS is based on fear and ignorance. AIDS victims are sometimes treated like social outcasts – 'lepers' like those described in the Bible. Parents kept their children away from one school in which a child was known to have the virus; some insurance companies charge high premiums to people known to be homosexual; church members have refused to share the chalice at Holy Communion with AIDS victims.

Many people look on AIDS as a 'judgement' from God – that is, a punishment for humankind's sins. Since AIDS is more prevalent among homosexuals, this reinforces people's prejudice against homosexuals as being unnatural or in some way 'sinful' (see Unit 2.8). AIDS has been nicknamed 'the gay plague'.

Such treatment is both cruel and unnecessary. As we have seen, it is not easy to catch AIDS. Victims and their families need support and understanding. Special units and hospices have been set up in some parts of the country to deal with AIDS sufferers.

What do we know about AIDS?

- The HIV virus seems to have originated in Africa. Scientists believe it may have developed in monkeys. So far, people with HIV virus have been found in 90 countries.
- No-one knows how many people worldwide have died from AIDS. The death-toll in USA and Europe at the moment is around 20,000. In the United Kingdom, by the end of 1987, about 50,000 people were known to carry the HIV virus, over 1200 had developed AIDS and 697 people had died. Experts predict that the illness will continue to spread at an alarming rate.
- About 90% of people with HIV in Western countries are homosexual. But in Africa, more than 50% of those affected are heterosexual. The disease is likely to spread more among the heterosexual population in the West, unless people change their sexual habits.
- There is clear evidence that homosexuals in this country have altered their sexual behaviour to combat AIDS – for example, having fewer sexual partners. But will heterosexuals do the same?

A matter of opinion

Opening a Conference of Health Ministers in London in 1988, the Princess Royal, Princess Anne, said:

The AIDS epidemic is a classic own goal by the human race, a self-inflicted wound that serves to remind homo sapiens of its own fallibility.

- This remark outraged many AIDS sufferers and carers. Do you think the Princess' remark would reinforce, or combat, prejudice against AIDS victims?

William Buckley, columnist with the *New York Times*, wrote recently:

Everyone detected with AIDS should be tattooed on the upper forearm to protect common needle users and on the buttocks to prevent the victimisation of other homosexuals.

- How do you react to this remark?

3.1 Why work?

A   *For this woman, work is a matter of survival.*

I hate getting up for work in the morning. My father has to drag me out of bed. I get to work just before 8 o'clock, clock in, have a fag and a cup of coffee and then go to see the foreman. The morning goes by in a sort of haze until lunchtime. At 12.30 I stop and eat my sandwiches – we only get 30 minutes break because of the bonus system. Then another two hours before the hooter goes and we all knock off. Within three minutes the entire factory is empty.

Rob, 19

Rob is one of 26 million people in paid employment in Britain today. Most of them are employed in one of three kinds of industry:

1 *Primary industries* which exploit natural resources, such as mining, agriculture and fishing. The number of jobs in these industries has declined dramatically in recent years.
2 *Secondary or manufacturing industries* – these include car production, electronics, chemicals etc
3 *Tertiary or service industries* which provide services such as banking, shops, estate agents and tourist facilities. The number of people involved in this kind of work has increased considerably since the Second World War.

Notice the words 'in paid employment'. The figure quoted doesn't include the millions of people who work long, hard hours for nothing. Parents of small children, housewives, those who care for elderly or sick relatives all 'work' but are not included in the numbers of the employed. It's easy to forget all the different types of work that go on in our society.

Why work?

If you asked Rob why he went to work, he'd probably say 'For the money'. But that is just one of the reasons why the majority of people want to work. Some of the others are:

1 To satisfy basic needs – for food, clothing and shelter. In most Western societies almost everyone earns or receives enough to cover these basic needs. But in much of the developing world this is far from true. For some, having a job and a wage (however small) can literally mean the difference between life and death (**A**).

In a developed country like Britain, which has a

26

high standard of living, it can be difficult to distinguish between a 'need' and a 'want'. Rob, for example, would say he 'needs' a car, new clothes, a video recorder ... The desire for a bigger house, a faster car, may make us work harder and longer hours, or seek a better-paid job – until, sometimes, we no longer have the leisure time to enjoy our new possessions.

---

1 Make a list of ten objects which you consider to be necessities and ten which your family regularly buy which are luxuries. Compare your list with a partner.

---

2   To achieve self-respect and personal satisfaction. Work, it seems, is an essential part of being human. A person's sense of identity is closely linked with his or her occupation. One of the first questions we ask a new acquaintance is 'What do you do?'. The danger, of course, is that we then judge that person according to their work, rather than who they are. Unemployment may lead to depression, loss of status and lack of enthusiasm for life. As one mother said:

Being out of work has made my son lazy. It is as much as he can do to get out of bed in the morning and dress himself. But he never used to be like that when he had a job ...

---

2 Do you think it is wrong to judge a person by what he or she does? What other 'measures' do we use to evaluate people (eg clothing/appearance; politeness; interests ...)

---

3   To gain a sense of achievement and fulfilment. For many people, like Rob, work represents boredom and drudgery. But for some – the lucky ones – it can give a great sense of satisfaction and achievement. Some Christians believe that *any* job, no matter how mundane, should be done as well as it possibly can be, and 'to the Glory of God' (see Unit 3.2).

---

3 Do you think it is possible to live up to the Christian ideal of work? How could a person find fulfilment in a boring factory job?

---

4   For contact with others. Many people enjoy the contact with their colleagues and the atmosphere of a busy working environment. For example, some parents with young children return to work because they need the stimulus of adult conversation.

---

4 Many unemployed people describe their feeling of isolation. What do you think they mean by this?

---

5   To maintain and control the environment. Many jobs bring people into direct contact with the world around them (eg farming, fishing, mining, irrigation work). From earliest times people have depended on the natural world – this remains true even in the modern 'scientific' age. The creation story in the Book of Genesis reinforces this:

B   Genesis 1.28
Be fruitful and multiply and fill the earth and subdue it.

In the story that follows we learn that humankind has always had to work hard. The first jobs were to do with agriculture:

C   Genesis 2.15
The Lord God took the man and put him in the Garden of Eden to till it and keep it.

---

5 What would happen if people did not work to control the environment?
6 Why is work so important to most people?

What does the Bible have to say?

2 Thessalonians 3.10
If any one will not work, let him not eat.

● Do you think this could apply in today's world?

Ecclesiastes 5.19
Every man also to whom God has given wealth and possessions and power to enjoy them, and to accept his lot and find enjoyment in his toil – this is the gift of God.

● What do you think makes a person happy in his or her work?

I Corinthians 4.11,12
To the present hour we hunger and thirst, we are ill-clad and buffetted and homeless, and we labour, working with our own hands.

● Does working hard necessarily bring wealth?

3.2 Work as a calling

I suppose, judging by most people's standards, I'm a bit of a failure! After all, I haven't got a car or a house, I earn much less than my contemporaries at home and my chances of promotion are virtually nil. But I get such satisfaction from my work – I really feel a sense of purpose – you know, that I'm where I ought to be. How many of my old school friends could say that?

Sunnita, a development worker

Many people would find Sunnita's attitude to work hard to understand. She clearly has no interest in financial gain or status – aspects of work that concern most of us. Although she doesn't use the word, Sunnita is expressing a sense of **vocation**, or a particular 'calling' to do her work.

What is a vocation?

You may have heard the word 'vocation' used in a religious context. People who enter a convent or monastery are said to have a 'religious vocation' – that is, they feel called by God to live as nuns or monks. Similarly, a person may feel that he or she has a calling to be a priest or a minister.

Nowadays, however, the word is also used to describe some more everyday occupations, in par-

A *What do you think this Oxfam worker gains from his job? Would you describe this as a vocation?*

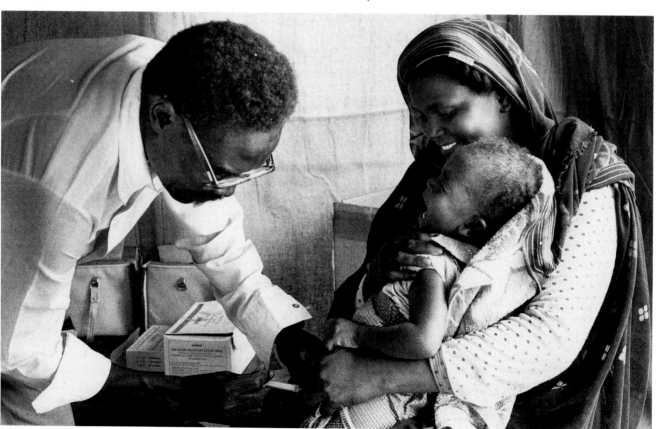

ticular the so-called 'caring' professions: nursing, teaching, social work (**A**). Some people may feel that God wants tham to become a doctor or a teacher. Many more take on this work in order to serve their fellow human beings, rather than because they have any religious belief.

Unfortunately, however, society sometimes under-values this sort of work. For Sunnita, the satisfaction of helping others is enough. But many involved in a caring 'vocation' feel taken-for-granted and resent their low pay. After all, as one nurse commented:

You can't live on job satisfaction! We spend our lives caring for the sick and suffering – but who looks after us?

In recent years there have been bitter disputes and strikes involving members of the caring professions, demanding better rates of pay and working conditions.

---

1 What other occupations would you describe as 'vocations'? Why?
2 'A vocation is its own reward'. Do you agree? Is it fair that people should have to choose between caring for others and personal gain?
3 Do you think that nurses, teachers, ambulance drivers etc should ever go on strike? Why?

The Christian attitude to work

Many Christians would use the word 'vocation' in a much wider sense. They believe that *all* people should do their work 'to the glory of God'. This means working as hard and as well as you can, whether you are filling tins with baked beans, working on a supermarket check-out, making high-level Government decisions or running in the Olympics! St Paul sums this up:

B Colossians, 3.23
Whatever you do, work at it with all your heart, as working for the Lord, not for men . . .

The Christian attitude to work also involves care and consideration for your fellow workers and an awareness of your *responsibilities* as a worker.

Rights and responsibilities

We hear a lot about workers' 'rights' – to good pay, good working conditions, longer holidays and

so on. But what about responsibilities? Both employers and employees have responsibilities towards each other. Often relationships become strained and a 'them' and 'us' situation develops. Yet the interests of both sides need not necessarily be in competition. Good employers will ensure that their workers are well paid and have good conditions; sensible employees want to work for a profitable and well-run company.

C looks at the rights and responsibilities of employers and employees.

C Right and responsibilities

The employer should ensure that:
- workers operate in safe, healthy conditions. Not every job can be made pleasant, but there should be no unnecessary risks
- employers are paid a fair wage and given sufficient holidays
- no-one is penalised on the grounds of colour, sex, race or religion
- there is a system by which workers can make complaints
- no-one is expected to work unreasonable hours, and workers have the right to withdraw their labour

The employee should:
- keep to the terms of their contract
- be honest with their employer's time and money
- be absent only when genuinely unable to work
- be prepared to do a fair day's work for a fair day's pay
- only withdraw labour (go on strike) after all attempts to settle a dispute have failed

---

4 Can you add any other responsibilities to the lists in **C**?
5 Do you agree with the Christian view of *all* work as a vocation? Can you think of any jobs which a Christian might not be willing to do?
6 Read the parable told by Jesus in Matthew 2, 1–16. What does this parable have to say about the rights and responsibilities of employers? What does it tell us about a Christian attitude to work?

29

3.3 Unemployment

When my Dad lost his job he became almost a different person. He lost interest in everything – the garden, his hobbies, his friends ... I think he felt he'd failed us all. He said going to the DHSS office was the most humiliating experience in his life ...
Diane, 14

For many people, like Diane's Dad, unemployment comes as a shattering blow. Along with their job, they lose self-esteem, interest and a sense of purpose in life. In the same way, for school leavers who cannot find a job, life seems to stretch ahead with no real purpose.

It is difficult to calculate exactly how many people are 'unemployed' at any one time. The 'official' figure for Spring 1989 was just under 2,000,000 unemployed. **A** shows variations in the unemployment rate 1971–1986.

However, these figures do not give us the full picture. Only people who receive State benefits and are registered to work are included. This does not include most married women, who cannot claim benefit if their husband is employed. If their husband is unemployed himself, the benefit is given in his name. The figures also exclude thousands of young people on training schemes, all unemployed men over the age of 60, and many of the 'down and outs' and others who live on the move.

---

1 Whenever a new set of unemployment figures is issued, the Government is accused of 'fixing' the statistics. Do you think it is easy – or even possible – to give the full picture? Why might a government prefer to show fewer unemployed?

Causes of unemployment

Most countries in the developed world have an unemployment problem, although the percentage of unemployed people varies considerably from

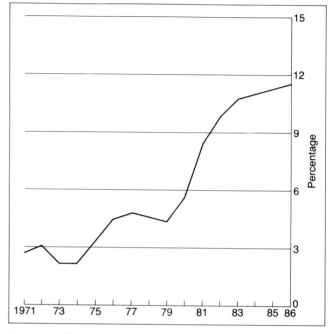

A *Unemployment 1971–1986. The figures show the percentage of the total population available for work (excluding school leavers).*

country to country. The main causes of unemployment in Britain are:

- a decline in manufacturing industry in the face of competition from overseas;
- increasing automation/mechanisation;
- a growth in the number of people seeking work – ie more competition for fewer jobs.

Tackling the problem

Different governments have tried various ways of overcoming the unemployment problem – with varying degrees of success. Ideas include:

1 *Government training schemes* These are aimed particularly at school leavers. They offer young people a chance to learn useful skills, and gain some experience of work. However, critics say

that the trainees are often exploited and used as 'cheap labour'; moreover, the young person has no guarantee that there will be a job at the end of their training;

2 *Re-training schemes* Re-training programmes are aimed at older members of the workforce who have become redundant. For example, someone of 45 who had worked in the declining steel industry could be re-trained to work, say, in catering. However, there is still a problem of getting a job at the end of the retraining.

3 *100% employment* In some countries, the government guarantees every person a job. This may sound ideal, but it puts a great strain on the economy of the country.

4 *Military service* Although the main purpose of military service is for defence, rather than employment, it may offer a temporary solution for school leavers. However, there is still the problem of finding jobs when young people leave the forces.

---

2 Choose one of the 'solutions' above and try and find out as much as you can about it – ie where it operates, who qualifies, how long schemes last. Then write a report on your research, and state whether you think the scheme is an answer to the unemployment problem.

Demographics

'Demographics' is the study of statistics concerning population change. Experts in demographics now tell us that the employment/unemployment picture is changing. Since the late 1960s, the birth rate (number of children born per 1000 of the population) has been declining. That means there are fewer young graduates and school leavers looking for jobs. Some experts predict that, far from competing for work, young people will be able to 'pick and choose' among employers by the year 2000. Companies will be keen to hold on to their older workers and encourage women to return to work when they have had their families.

---

3 Experts predict that by the year 2000 we will have an 'ageing' population – ie, that there will be a higher proportion of old people. What effects do you think this will have in the workplace?

The human factor

When we hear about statistics, unemployment rates, 'the workforce' it's easy to forget that each statistic is a person. Different people react to unemployment in different ways. Some are able to use their 'enforced leisure' constructively: they may take up new hobbies or spare-time interests; do voluntary work; join a club. Others, however, find it very difficult to cope with life without a job. The following problems have been blamed on unemployment:

- low morale, depression, poor self-esteem, even suicide;
- tension within families;
- marital break-down;
- an increase in drug-taking and alcohol abuse;
- an increase in crime;
- inner city problems such as vandalism, violence – even rioting;
- racial abuse and attacks.

---

4 Can the above problems be blamed on unemployment, or is this just an 'excuse'? Give reasons for your answer.
5 What answer – if any – do you think Christianity can offer the unemployed?

What does the Bible say?

Unemployment clearly wasn't a problem in Biblical times. If a person did not work, it was assumed that he was lazy:

2 Thessalonians 3.6,10
'keep away from every brother who is living in idleness
If anyone will not work let him not eat.'

A matter of opinion

You've only got to open the paper to see dozens of vacancies … and then these scroungers say they can't get a job. The trouble with this country is that we're too soft – all these benefits and handouts. We never had them in my day. If they won't work, let them starve, that's what I say.

- Do you agree with this opinion? Give you reasons.
- Act out the conversation between the speaker and an unemployed school leaver.

3.4 Money

A *A lucky man – or is he?*

Have you ever dreamt of winning the pools, like the man in **A**, or becoming a millionaire? How would you spend your money? Would you buy a huge house, a fast car, exotic holidays ...? It's tempting to think that money can solve all our problems. But does it?

---

1 What would *you* do if you won the pools? Do you think you would be happier if you had more money? What problems might you face?

Until around the seventh century BC, most people were able to obtain what they wanted by bartering or payment in kind. For example, if you needed a new cooking pot, you might ask the village potter to make it, in exchange for some grain, or eggs ... That way, you had your pot, and the potter obtained food. Some societies still rely on bartering to a large extent.

Gradually, however, the system became more complicated. People began to exchange food and other items for small pieces of metal, of standard shape and weight – and so coins were born.

Nowadays, coins are just one of the 'symbols' used in everyday transactions. In addition, there are notes, cheques, credit cards, postal orders.

---

2 What do you think would happen if Britain returned to a system of barter? Do you think it could work?

How do people acquire money?

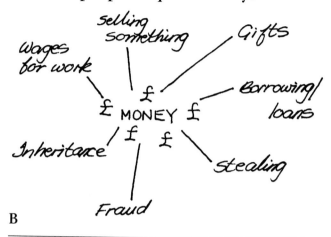

B

---

3 Can you think of any other means of getting money? Would you accept money from all these sources? If not, why not?

What does the Bible say?

Matthew 6.24
(Jesus said) *'No one can serve two masters; for either he will hate the one and love the other, or he will be devoted to the one and despise the other. You cannot serve God and mammon (money).'*

● What do you think Jesus meant by describing money as a 'master'?

1 Timothy 6.9–10
But those who desire to be rich fall into temptation, into a snare, into many senseless and hurtful desires that plunge men into ruin and destruction. For the love of money is the root of all evils ...

● Do you agree that the love of money is the root of all evils?

A matter of opinion

There's nothing wrong with money itself. It's what people do with money – and what money does to them – that causes the problems.

● What do you think the speaker meant? Do you agree? Explain your answer.

3.5 Debt

I was robbing Peter to pay Paul and borrowing more and more from the moneylender. I would pay him off what I could and then he would say, "Look, you owe me £20, how about borrowing another £50 and I'll take the £20 off that." That meant I had some money in hand for Christmas presents, or if the children needed clothes. It makes your problems worse in the long run, but it helps at the time when you are badly pushed. I was also buying things from mail-order catalogues, paying the lady who collected on the estate bit by bit.

Everyone thought I was managing very well: no-one knew what was really going on. The children were happy, well-fed, always looked neat and clean. I didn't want anyone to know. If my dad had known that my jewellery was in the pawnshop and we were so deeply in debt, he'd have gone berserk. He would have given us all his savings. But that would have been the easy way out.

I felt that whatever happened I musn't miss the moneylender or paying the court order because I thought that if I did that, it would be the end of everything. They would send the bailiffs in to take away our things.

Carole, 35

What's your idea of a typical 'debtor' — someone who goes on wild spending sprees? A gambler (see Unit 7.6)? A shiftless scrounger? Someone irresponsible who simply cannot manage money? None of these descriptions would apply to Carole, yet when her husband lost his job she became trapped in a spiral of debt and deceit.

Early in 1989 the Citizen's Advice Bureau reported that it now advises more people about debt problems than anything else. The average family is now in debt to six different companies and carries three credit cards.

It has never been so easy to borrow money. Banks and building societies offer personal loans. Most people have credit cards which enable them to 'buy now and pay later'. Every High Street store offers the possibility of payments in a number of 'easy' instalments — on anything from furniture to clothing or a car.

Why do people get into debt?

Often a combination of factors rather than one single cause leads a person into debt. Major causes include:

- very low income;
- difficulty in managing money;
- temptation to buy more than they can afford;
- family difficulties (eg redundancy);
- ease of obtaining credit.

1 Do you think it is too easy to obtain credit? Would you consider buying something on hire purchase? Why/why not?

Who can help?

Carole went to her local Citizen's Advice Bureau. They gave her legal advice and helped her work out a budget plan to pay off her debts over a long period.

2 Do you think people like Carole deserve help? Or should they face the consequences of their own mistakes? Explain your answer.

What does the Bible have to say?

Read Matthew 18.23–35

- Do you think Jesus was only talking about money? What other sorts of 'debts' can you think of?

A matter of opinion

'Buy now, pay laterr' is the motto of the twentieth century.

- Do you agree? What problems does this attitude cause?

3.6 Leisure

What do you do with your spare time?

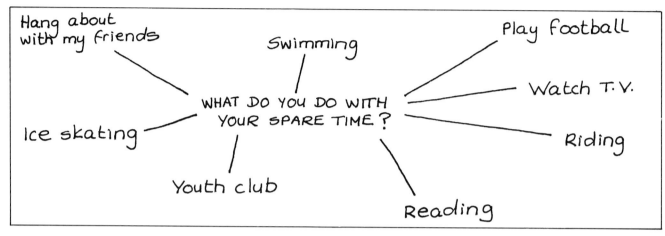

Hang about with my friends

Swimming

Play football

WHAT DO YOU DO WITH YOUR SPARE TIME?

Watch T.V.

Ice skating

Riding

Youth club

Reading

A

These are just a few of the ways in which people spend their leisure time. Your own list might include some of these, or it might be completely different.

Experts suggest that we need a balance of 'work, rest and play' in order to keep healthy and enjoy life. Too much of one element is bad for us – for example the person who works all the time may suffer from stress and anxiety; the person who 'rests' all the time is not leading a healthy life.

The dictionary defines leisure as 'time at one's own disposal' – that is, the time when *you* can choose what you want to do. Of course, a number of factors affect how we spend our leisure time:

1 Money (or lack of it)
2 Local facilities
3 Age
4 Physical ability and health

The five ages of leisure

People's leisure activities change as they grow older. For example, you probably wouldn't include 'gardening' as one of your spare-time activities, but your parents or grandparents might. **B** is one way of looking at the five 'ages' of leisure.

B   The five 'ages' of leisure
1 Childhood/teenage – playing with friends; sporting activities; watching TV
2 Early married life – leisure activities centred around setting up home, having children ... DIY; indoor hobbies; cooking; gardening
3 35–45 – more time spent outside the home with friends – eating out, church and small group activities, dinners and dances, foreign holidays
4 Middle age – eating out, clubs such as golf/bridge, holidays
5 Old age – knitting, gardening, walking, visiting social club

1 Draw up a chart like **B** based on the leisure interests of people you know in the different age groups. How is their use of leisure time affected by: money, local facilities, health?

C *No money and nothing to do. Is this a good use of leisure time?*

Increasing amounts of leisure time

Most people in Britain today have far more leisure time than people did a century ago. The average working week is now less than 40 hours – whereas about 100 years ago, some people worked an 80 hour week.

Statistics can be misleading, however. Some people – for example, mothers with young children or those caring for elderly or disabled relatives – have little or no leisure time.

Moreover, the idea of 'leisure' is meaningless to many people in the world's developing countries, who have to work long hours in poor conditions simply to survive.

---

2 Why is it misleading to talk about people having more leisure time?

'Enforced' leisure

Unlimited leisure time may sound like a dream come true – but for many people it is more like a nightmare. For the unemployed, the retired, or those unable to work, too much leisure time can lead to boredom, frustration and depression – especially as they may have no money to spare for hobbies and spare-time activities. Boredom and 'enforced' leisure are often blamed for vandalism and increasing crime rates.

---

3 What would you do if you had unlimited leisure? Do you think you might encounter problems in filling the time? What local facilities could you use (eg sports club, social club, parks ...)? How could the local council cater more for people's leisure needs?

4 Why is leisure important? What would you say is a 'good' use of leisure? What is a 'bad' use?

5 Most people in the developed world now have more leisure time than their fathers or grandfathers dreamt of. Draw up a chart listing the advantages and disadvantages of increased leisure time.

What does the Bible say?

Genesis 2.2–4
And on the seventh day God finished his work which he had done, and he rested on the seventh day from all his work which he had done. So God blessed the seventh day and hallowed it, because on it God rested from all his work which he had done in creation.

Exodus 20.8
Remember the Sabbath day, to keep it holy. Six days you shall labour and do all your work; but the seventh day is a sabbath to the Lord your God; in it you shall not do any work.

● Do you think Sunday (the Sabbath) should be a special 'day of rest' or a working day like any other? Give your reasons.

A matter of opinion

The United Nations *Declaration of Human Rights* (see Unit 9.2) states:

Everyone has the right to rest and leisure, including reasonable working hours and holidays with pay.

● Do you think that everyone has a 'right' to leisure time?
● Does everyone in this country enjoy this right?

DISCRIMINATION

4.1 What is race?

Do you know the one about the Englishman, the Irishman, the Scotsman and the Welshman ..?

You've probably heard a lot of jokes that begin like this. They usually go on to mention the so-called 'characteristics' of a particular race – all Irishmen are stupid, all Scots are mean, the English all have 'stiff upper lips' .. and so on. Harmless fun? Or is this a form of racism?

---

1 Do you think these jokes are racist? Why/why not?

By way of definition

- The Oxford English Dictionary defines *racism* (or, less commonly, racialism) as:

  Belief in superiority of a particular race; antagonism between different races.

  At its most extreme, this 'antagonism' can lead to hatred, violence and oppression.

- *Prejudice* literally means 'pre-judging' someone, without giving them the benefit of the doubt, and without knowing the facts about a situation. Of course, everyone has the right to choose their friends – but if that choice is made on the basis of an ignorant dislike of members of a different race, it is rooted in prejudice.

  'Colour prejudice' is a dislike of someone else simply because of the colour of their skin.

- *Discrimination* often results from prejudice. If people are treated unfairly simply because of their race, they are being discriminated against. Many countries pass laws to try and ensure that all people are treated equally.

- *Stereotyping* is a form of discrimination in which all members of a particular group, or race, are thought to share certain characteristics. For example:

'All West Indians are good at sport.'

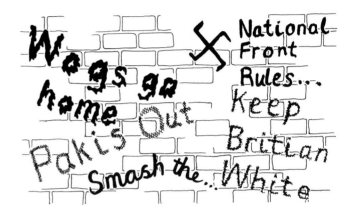

A *Racism can take many forms.*

B *A victim of Nazi persecution in pre-war Germany.*

'All Indians work hard.'
'All Africans have a good sense of rhythm.'

Even positive statements like these are stereotypical. But often the so-called 'typical' characteristics are far from desirable, and form the basis for racist abuse and name calling.

---

2 Is your generation prejudiced against any particular group? If so, can you think why?

36

What causes racism?

For long periods in evolution, geographical barriers (oceans, deserts, mountain ranges) kept different groups apart. As a result, each group or race developed its own characteristics: of size and stature, physical features, and colour.

Like most other animals, human beings feel safest when those around them are the same as themselves. Any 'outsider' is seen as a threat, anything different is viewed with suspicion and fear. This fear – based on ignorance – lies at the root of racism.

Of course, most people would deny that they are 'afraid'. They justify their prejudice by saying that the outsiders will take their jobs, buy up all the houses, follow a strange way of life ... in other words, they aren't 'like us'. Often these fears and suspicions lie dormant, only to be stirred up when there is an incident or problem.

Prejudice is not always directed by individuals against other individuals. In Germany, for example, the Nazis worked up so much hatred against the Jews that they were able to murder millions with very little opposition. In South Africa, the Government maintains a system of *apartheid* which discriminates against the rights of black people (see Unit 4.3).

---

3 In the next week, watch TV and look in newspapers for articles on racism, or incidents where you think some sort of racism is involved. Try to work out the *causes* of the conflict.

A matter of opinion

Most of the people I know would deny that they are the slightest bit racist. They pride themselves on being tolerant and open minded. But when I introduce my fiance, Kofi, who's black, their reactions give them away. Some are simply struck dumb. Others are embarrassed. And some are downright insulting ...

● Do you think that racism is a problem in Britain? What more could be done to overcome it?

4.2 The Black Community in Britain

The other day someone said to me, 'Why don't you go back home, to your own country?' I was furious – this is my country. I was born here. I've never even been to Jamaica. And I've got just as much right to be here as she has.

Melanie, 17

Melanie is a second-generation immigrant. Her parents came to Britain from the West Indies in the early 1960s and her father got a job in the steel industry. Her mother followed, and Melanie and her brothers were born in Britain. They are all British citizens. But many white people find this hard to accept.

A nation of settlers

Who *are* the British? In fact, people have been coming to settle in Britain for so many centuries that we are *all* descended from immigrants! Viking, Roman and Norman invaders all mingled with the early inhabitants of the islands and left their mark on the language, the landscape and the 'national' characteristics.

Over the centuries immigrants have come to Britain for two main reasons:

1 To work – for example, during the 19th century many Irish people came to work in the

A *Relations between black and white are not always so relaxed. What ways of combatting racism can you suggest?*

construction industry; in the 1950 and '60s the British Government encouraged people from the West Indies (like Melanie's father) to come and work in Britain.

2　To escape persecution – many Jews and Poles fled to Britain before and during the Second World War; in the 1970s Asians who were expelled from Uganda found refuge in Britain; 'boat people' came from Vietnam, Kurds from Turkey.

Coloured immigrants began to come to Britain from the countries of the Empire in the 1920s and '30s. After the Second World War many more came, mainly from the West Indies, India and Pakistan. Some found it difficult to find homes. They moved into the poorer areas of cities like Manchester, Birmingham and London. As friends and relatives arrived they, too, settled in these areas, and ethnic communities grew up.

Today there are around 2.5 million coloured people in Britain – that's about 4% of the total population. New tougher legislation has been introduced which has limited the numbers of immigrants allowed into the country.

1　Why do you think the British government was keen to welcome immigrants during the 1950s and '60s?
2　Find out as much as you can about present government policy on immigration. Do you think it is fair? Explain your answer.

The law

As we saw in the last unit, many black people face prejudice, abuse and discrimination. In 1976 the British Government passed the Race Relations Act. This was intended to protect every citizen in Britain from racial discrimination. It means that if a coloured person applies for a job, rents a flat, buys something in a shop, is a student, an employee or a tenant, he or she has exactly the same rights *under law* as a white person. If the coloured person has evidence of discrimination, he or she could take legal action.

The Race Relations Act also makes 'incitement to racial hatred' an offence.

---

3 a) Explain how racial discrimination might apply in the following situations:

- two candidates apply for a job; both have similar qualifications, but one is black and one white; the white person gets the job.
- a landlord advertises a vacancy in a flat. When a black person comes to look at it, she is told that the flat has gone.
- a black warehouse assistant always has to sweep the floor – his white colleagues never have to.

b) How easy do you think it would be for a black person to *prove* discrimination in each case? What might stop a person complaining, even though they felt they were being discriminated against?

4 Is it ever possible to change people's attitudes by passing laws?

5 Photograph **A** was taken at London's Notting Hill Carnival, a day when whites and blacks celebrate together. What can the individual do to help overcome racism?

The Race Relations Act was a major step towards improving the situation of black people in Britain. But how effective has it been? In 1985 a Social Attitudes Survey found that 35% of white people questioned were prepared to describe themselves as racially prejudiced (how many more were unwilling to admit this?). 66% of black people in the survey felt that they had been refused a job because of their colour.

A Christian responsibility?

Christians believe that everyone is equal in God's family. Therefore no person or race can be inferior mentally, physically or spiritually, to another.

B Galatians, 3.28
There is neither Jew nor Greek, slave nor free, male nor female, for you are all one in Christ Jesus.

Belief is one thing – practice another. Christians very often fail to live up to this ideal. In the past,

some Christian missionaries persecuted and killed other races in the name of religion. In the sixteenth century, Spanish conquistadores invaded South America. They enslaved the native Indians, took their land, and forced them to become Christian. Those who refused were tortured and killed.

In South Africa today the Dutch Reformed Church upholds the racialist policy of apartheid (see Unit 4.3).

Christians are guilty of prejudice and intolerance in this country, too. Many of the West Indians who came to Britain in the 1950s and '60s were Christian. But they received a poor welcome in British churches. Groups set up churches of their own. It is ironic that these 'black' churches continue to grow and flourish, while many of the old-established churches have dwindling congregations.

---

6 Jesus himself came from the Middle East. Yet most Western art portrays him as white and European. Why do you think this is?

7 A Nigerian student wrote:
God is black, a beautiful shining black. It is a wicked white man's lie to say that he is white. The Devil is white.

a) What was your first reaction to these words?

b) What was the student trying to say?

c) Do you agree with him?

A matter of opinion:

How often have you heard statements like these:

They come here and steal our jobs ... why don't they go back home?

I wouldn't object to my daughter marrying a white man – but mixed marriages never work. And the children always suffer ...

I think the immigrants themselves are to blame – after all, they don't make any effort to fit in with our ways, do they? They go on talking their own language and wearing their own clothes, and then complain that they are not accepted!

How can we let our daughter go out with her white friends? She is a good, religious girl. Their clothes are indecent, they smoke and drink. The young people in this country have no moral standards.

- For each statement, say:
  a) If you agree or disagree, and why.
  b) Who you think might make such a statement, and what their real feelings are.
  c) How you would reply.

DISCRIMINATION
4.3 South Africa

The whole world tries to tell us how to run our lives. But how many people come to South Africa to find out for themselves what it's like? I maintain that apartheid is the best system for this country. Blacks simply don't have the education – or the ability – to govern. It's all very well for you to talk about equal rights – most blacks wouldn't know what to do with them if they had them!

Pieter, a white Afrikaaner

The population of South Africa is made up of four major groups (**A**).

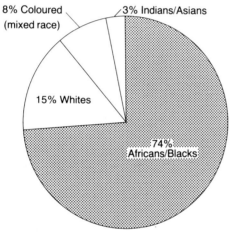

A *The population of South Africa. Which racial group is in the majority?*

You can see from **A** that the majority of the population is black. Yet all the power and privilege in South Africa rests in the hands of whites, like Pieter – although they make up only 15% of the population. The South African government maintains this unfair situation through the system of **apartheid**: officially described as the 'separate development' of whites and blacks.

What is apartheid?

Oppression of the black people in South Africa began well over 100 years ago when European settlers colonised the area. They took over the land and employed black people, at very low wages, to labour in the mines and industries. South Africa exports diamonds, coal, gold, fruit and wine – but black workers get almost nothing of the wealth they help to create. White people own 87% of the land in South Africa.

In 1948 the South African government set up the system of apartheid which reinforced this gap between the white, privileged minority and the black majority. The system included laws which:

- excluded blacks from certain cinemas, buses, schools and hospitals for 'whites only';
- allowed local councils to designate park benches and beaches 'whites only' (**B**);
- made marriage or sex between black and white illegal;
- confined blacks to 'homelands' in certain parts of the country.

Black people do not have the right to vote, so they were – and still are – powerless to change this unfair system.

Some of the petty restrictions have been lifted since then, but the homelands policy continues. Between 1960 and 1984 some 3,500,000 black Africans were forcibly evicted from their homes and sent to re-settlement areas called homelands or Bantustans. Some were forced out because whites claimed their land, others were evicted when their labour was no longer needed. The government argued that the blacks were being returned to their traditional, tribal lands.

About 40% of all South African blacks now live in the homelands. These areas are often the least fertile parts of the country. Jobs are scarce, but most people are not allowed to leave their homeland in search of work. Many families are split up: the men working in the cities, their wives and children living on a homeland miles away.

Some Africans have jobs in the major cities and live in townships such as Soweto (on the edge of Johannesburg) and Crossroads (outside Cape Town). Since 1948 all Africans living outside the homelands have had to carry identity cards – they are treated as aliens in their own country.

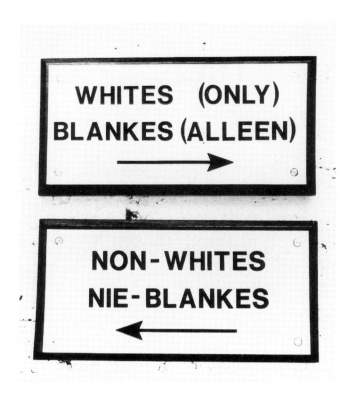

B *Signs like this may have disappeared in South Africa, but the system of apartheid remains.*

In recent years there have been many riots and violent protests in South Africa against government oppression. These have been harshly crushed by government forces.

---

1 Why do you think the unfair system of apartheid has been able to continue for so long in South Africa?

The rights and wrongs

Almost the whole world condemns South Africa for its policy of apartheid. The United Nations has declared its opposition to the system. Many countries have broken diplomatic and sporting links with South Africa. Some countries refuse to import South African products.

Opponents of apartheid – inside and outside South Africa – condemn it for perpetuating a system whereby the white minority possesses 87% of the land and enjoys a privileged lifestyle, with good wages, high standards of health care and education. They argue that this privilege is gained by exploiting black people.

Supporters of apartheid claim that the white settlers have made South Africa into the richest African country. They maintain that blacks also benefit from this and have a higher standard of living than black people anywhere else in Southern Africa. The policy of apartheid, they say, enables both blacks and whites to enjoy their own culture and way of life.

---

2 Hold a class debate between supporters and opponents of apartheid.
3 Find out as much as you can about the situation in South Africa today. Do you think there is hope for a more equal system?

What does the Bible say?

Numbers 15.15
... there shall be one statute (rule) *for you and for the stranger who sojourns* (stays) *with you ... One law ... shall be for you and for the stranger who sojourns with you.*

● Who *is* the stranger in South Africa?

Acts 10.34,35
And Peter opened his mouth and said: 'Truly I perceive that God shows no partiality (favouritism), but in every nation any one who fears him and does what is right is acceptable to him.'

● Do you think it is possible for a Christian to support apartheid?

A matter of opinion

South Africans must do what they see fit in their own country. It's no-one else's business.

White people and black people in South Africa have very different histories and different ideas about living. It's in everybody's interests to keep the two apart.

Most black people are happy about the way they are treated. Only trouble makers try to stir up protest. Why should we change?

All people, whatever their colour, are equal and should be treated equally.

It is totally wrong for the white minority to govern this country, to posses so much of its land and own so much of its wealth.

● For each of these statements, say whether you agree or disagree, and why.

41

4.4 Archbishop Desmond Tutu

A *Bishop Desmond Tutu.*

parish on the outskirts of Johannesburg. One day, Desmond and his mother passed the clergyman in the street. Huddleston raised his hat to Tutu's mother. You might not think there was anything odd about this – apart from being a little old-fashioned. But most whites treated blacks with contempt, regarding them almost as slaves. This simple action was one of the factors that prompted Tutu to begin his struggle against apartheid (**B**).

B *The problem of our country . . . is apartheid, it is injustice and oppression . . . we too are just ordinary human beings. We too love to be with our wives everyday. We too want our children to rush out to meet us as we come back from work. We too want to be able to move freely everywhere in the land of our birth. We too want to have security of tenure. We too want to participate in the decisions which affect our lives. These are not extravagant demands. They are the expectation of any human being. We want to have a new kind of South Africa, where we all, black and white, can walk together, black and white, into the glorious future which God is opening up before us.*

Archbishop Desmond Tutu (**A**) is famous throughout the world. He is an outspoken critic of apartheid and the South African government, and is also a leading churchman. Desmond Tutu is black – so he is discriminated against like all other black South Africans. His passport has been taken away on more than one occasion. But, perhaps because he is so famous, Desmond Tutu has not been imprisoned and silenced like another well-known critic of apartheid, Nelson Mandela.

'An event of some small significance'

When Desmond Tutu was a small boy, a white clergyman – Trevor Huddleston – had an African

1 What qualities do you think lead an individual like Desmond Tutu to fight against seemingly overwhelming odds?
2 Briefly sum up, in your own words, what Desmond Tutu was saying in **B**.

After he was ordained Desmond Tutu worked for some time in England. He returned to Africa in the mid-1970s, to find that the position of blacks in South Africa was becoming more and more intolerable. In 1976, Tutu wrote to the Prime Minister of South Africa, Mr Vorster. He warned that violence could break out in the black townships at any time.

In June 1976 the threatened violence erupted.

The trigger was a government decision that half of all school subjects should be taught in Afrikaans – the language of white South Africans. Pupils in the black township at Soweto organised a protest march on 16 June. The march was met by police, who threw tear-gas and then opened fire on the students – many of them no more than children (C). Later, reports differed over whether the police or the students started the violence. Many students were killed on that day and in the violence and rioting that followed. Again, it is difficult to find out how many died – some sources say 25, others 100.

Lawlessness spread through the townships. Rival groups fought each other. Anyone thought to be 'collaborating' with the white authorities risked death: sometimes being burnt alive in horrific 'necklace' killings. South Africa appeared to be on the brink of civil war, but the authorities took no action.

Desmond Tutu called on the rest of the world to force the South African government to abandon the system of apartheid. He asked other countries to impose *sanctions* (to withold supplies of fuel and other essential commodities) and to *boycott* (refuse to buy) South African goods.

Some countries responded to Tutu's plea. Others, including Britain, argued that taking action against the South African government would harm the black population most of all. Because some countries are still willing to trade with South Africa, the use of sanctions has so far been ineffective.

C   *The first victims of the Soweto Uprising in 1976. Many of those involved were schoolchildren.*

The use of violence

At the start of his campaign, Desmond Tutu condemned the use of violence. He supported the idea of non-violent protest (see Unit 6.3). Recently, however, some people think that Tutu's attitude towards violence has changed, and that he now accepts it as inevitable. In a BBC television interview in 1986, he stated:

I am not a pacifist. I am just a peacemaker.

---

3 What do you think Desmond Tutu meant by describing himself as a 'peacemaker'?
4 Could Christians support the use of violence to overthrow the system of apartheid?

---

5 Hold a class debate on the motion:
'This house believes that the British government is right not to impose sanctions on South Africa.' Try to find out as much as you can about the Government's policy towards South Africa. Then present your arguments for or against the use of sanctions.

A matter of opinion

They may remove a Tutu, they may remove the South African Council of Churches, but God's intention to establish his Kingdom of justice, of love, of compassion, will not be thwarted.

Desmond Tutu, 1982

● Do you think this is a hopeful statement? Why/why not?
● Explain what it means, in your own words.

DISCRIMINATION

4.5 Anti-Semitism

There are lots of Jewish people in this part of London – there is a synagogue just down the road, and some shops sell special kosher food. But they are just the same as everyone else. Why have they been hated and persecuted for centuries? I don't understand it.

James, 15

Most people in Britain today have heard about the horrors of Nazi concentration camps and the mass extermination of Jews during the Second World War. And most would say that it could never happen again – certainly not *here*. But could it?

Throughout history, it seems, the Jews have been persecuted, expelled from their homes, discriminated against and even murdered. Why should such hatred or *Anti-Semitism* be directed against the Jews?

As we saw in the section on race (Unit 4.1) much prejudice and racial hatred is based on fear and suspicion of anything different. The Jewish way of life has always set them apart from non-Jewish (Gentile) people:

- the Jews have always seen themselves as God's 'chosen people', with a special relationship with God. In the Old Testament book of Exodus, Moses was inspired by God to lead the Israelites (the Jews) out of slavery in Egypt to their own 'promised land' of Israel.
- over the centuries many laws and traditions developed: about prayer, food, cleanliness. For example, the Jewish Sabbath (Saturday) is a very special day, which involves prayers and a family meal.
- some Christians have blamed the Jews for bringing about the death of Jesus. They base this accusation on the words of the mob in the court of Pontius Pilate: 'His blood be on us and on our children!'
- like most other racial groups, many Jews have distinctive features which have been ridiculed and caricatured;
- traditionally, Jews have been successful in business and commerce. This provoked envy and suspicion.

44

1 Do you find it surprising that the Jews have been persecuted? Give your reasons.

Nazism and the Jews

In Hitler's Germany, the Jews were singled out for blame and hatred. The Nazis claimed that the Jews would threaten the 'purity' of the German race. The persecution began in minor ways:

- some teachers humiliated Jewish children in school;
- German people refused to buy goods in Jewish-owned shops;
- patients could not be treated by Jewish doctors;
- laws were passed forbidding marriage between Jews and non-Jews.

Gradually, however, the oppression of the Jews grew more violent. Jewish shops and synagogues were attacked. Jews were forced to wear yellow stars on their clothes. Many were arrested and put into concentration camps.

The 'final solution' to the Jewish problem, as the Nazis saw it, came when millions of Jews (about 6,000,000) were killed in extermination camps.

2 Very few people protested against the murder of the Jews. Many of them claimed not to know what was going on. Do you think this was the case? Or do you think it is possible for people to be blinded by hatred?

The land of Israel

The truth about what had happened shocked the world. As a result, the nation of Israel was created, as a 'homeland' for the Jews. To create this new country, land was taken from the Palestinian Arabs. What began as the solution to one conflict sowed the seeds of another, tragic war which still continues.

5.1 Growing old

A *Is this your picture of old age? How do you react to this photograph?*

Exodus 20.12
Honour your father and your mother . . .

1 Timothy 5.4
If a widow has children or grandchildren, let them first learn their religious duty to their own family and make some return to their parents . . .

Is this how you see old age? Do you think younger people should look after the old and respect them? Or do you feel more like Khalid:

I dread the thought of growing old. Feeble, rheumatic – maybe even senile – either you're a burden on your family, or you sit in some dreary old folks home waiting to die!

Old age – now and then

The place old people occupy in society has changed a great deal since Biblical times – and even since the beginning of this century.

Traditionally, old people have been cared for within the extended family (see Unit 1.1). Younger members of the family were taught to respect them and see them as possessors of wisdom, based on many years of experience. This is still the case for some societies and cultures.

Today, however, many old people are made to feel 'in the way'. Far from being treated with respect and dignity they may be patronised or even ridiculed. In today's fast-changing world, the experience of 50 or even 20 years ago may seem to have little to offer young people.

---

1 What do you think it means to honour and care for your parents and grandparents?
2 People sometimes talk about the modern 'youth culture'. What do you think this means? What does it suggest about the place of old people in our society?

B Old age – the facts

1 *Life expectancy* – in the UK a man can expect to live to the age of 69, a woman to 74. Of course, these are average figures – many people live well into their 70s and 80s.
2 *An ageing population* – there are over 10,000,000 retired people in the UK – about 17% of the total population. There are now over four times as many people over the age of 65 as there were in 1900. Statistics suggest that this trend is going to continue.
3 *Health care* – elderly people make heavier demands on the medical services than any other age group, A person of 70, for instance, is likely to visit the doctor seven times more often than someone in their 30s.
4 *Retirement* – the 'official' retirement age is 60 for women and 65 for men. At this age, people become eligible for the Old Age Pension. Many people continue to work beyond retirement age, whilst others take 'early retirement' in their late 50s. The state pension is only about 30% of the average working wage. Many old people find it difficult to make ends meet.
5 *Finance* – those who do not work (mainly young children and old people) must be supported by those who do. In the UK, employed people pay taxes which help provide essential services. In the mid-1980s about 37% of the population was not of working age. This proportion is likely to increase.

---

3 Does the prospect of an increasingly ageing population pose any problems for society? How do you think these might be overcome?

Growing old – end or beginning?

Most of us dread the thought of growing old for three main reasons:

1 Poverty – most elderly people experience a drop in income. Those entirely dependent on a state pension sometimes find it difficult to make ends meet.
2 Ill health – elderly people are more prone to chronic illnesses such as arthritis, rheumatism, bronchitis. It also takes them longer to recover from everyday illnesses such as flu, or from accidents.
3 Loneliness – many people (especially women) have to face old age alone when their partners die. Over 2,000,000 elderly people in the UK live on their own.

Many people, however, actively enjoy their old age. Improved standards of health care mean that many people are fit and active when they retire. Far from 'sitting around waiting to die' many elderly people take on a new lease of life, developing new interests and activities. For some, it is a chance to take up new studies, to travel, or simply devote more time to hobbies such as gardening or painting.

Old age may also bring a deep sense of peace and tranquility. As one old lady commented:

You no longer care what people think. You haven't got to struggle to get on, make a living . . . you can take each day as it comes and live it to the full.

For Christians, old age can be a time of spiritual growth and preparation for death.

---

4 What do you dread most about growing old?
5 Some experts suggest that as the proportion of old people in our society increases, it will become 'fashionable' to be old and more resources will be devoted to this age-group. What do you think?

Providing for the elderly

Provision for the elderly usually comes from two sources:

1 *The family* The modern family tends to be widely scattered. This may make it difficult for children to share the responsibility of caring for an elderly parent. What often happens is that one child (frequently an unmarried daughter) takes on the duty of caring for their parent(s). Or the old person is 'passed around' from child to child, and may feel hurt and unwanted.

Some communities, however, such as Jews, Hindus and Muslims, have much stronger family ties and emphasise the importance of caring for the old.

2 *The community* Many old people do not have close family ties. Not every family is able to look after older relatives. The wider community must therefore take on responsibility for looking after its elderly members. Ways in which the community cares for the old include: council homes or sheltered housing; services such as 'meals on wheels', clubs (see **A**) and day centres; free or reduced travel; reduced entrance fees; home-help services.

3 *Charities* such as Age Concern (**C**) and Help the Aged. **D** comes from the aims of Age Concern.

D *Age Concern England aims to enable elderly people to: retain the maximum possible choice over the direction of their lives; maintain good health throughout their later years; have continuing access to satisfying personal relationships; live in physical environments suited to their changing needs; and have as many opportunities as possible for involvement in fulfilling community and leisure activities.*

---

6 Do you think the responsibility for caring for the old should fall on the community? Or do you think families should be forced to do more?
7 Do you think enough is done to care for old people in this country? If not, what more is needed?
8 What do you think a Christian response to caring for the elderly should be?

A matter of opinion

Four views of old age:

Old age is . . . a lot of crossed-off names in an address book.   Ronald Blythe, *A View in Winter*

*When I am an old woman I shall wear purple
With a red hat which doesn't go, and doesn't suit me,
And I shall spend my pension on brandy and summer gloves
And satin sandals, and say we've no money for butter.*

Jenny Joseph   *Warning*

*Now all the world she knows is dead,
In this small room she lives her days,
The wash-hand stand and single bed,
Screened from the public gaze.*

John Betjeman   *A Few Late Chrysanthemums*

*Old age should burn and rage at close of day,
Rage, rage against the dying of the light.*
Dylan Thomas   *Do not gently into that good night*

- Choose two of these passages and explain
  a) What you think the writer was trying to say about old age.
  b) How the passage makes you feel.
- Write a passage or poem giving your own view of old age.

C

AGE TOWARDS A BRIGHTER FUTURE

AGE CONCERN ENGLAND ANNUAL REPORT 1987/88

5.2 Looking after the disabled

Until my car accident four years ago, I'd never thought much about the needs of the disabled. I didn't realise how difficult it is to do ordinary things like going shopping or visiting friends when you're in a wheelchair.

Around here the situation is improving. The council has built several toilets for the disabled and a lot of shops now have ramps and lifts. But it's people's attitudes we really need to change.

Mandy, 24

If you have ever broken an arm or a leg, you'll have had a glimpse of what it's like to be disabled.

---

1 What do you think Mandy meant about changing people's attitudes? Do you agree?
2 What could be done to educate the able-bodied about the needs of the disabled?

A Disability – the facts

- In Britain 1 in every 10 people suffers from some kind of permanent disability. The majority of these do not need any specialist help.
- 500,000 people in this country are mentally handicapped.
- There are about 1,200,000 disabled people in the UK who need some kind of help in order to live a normal life.

Around 60% of the world's disabled people live in developing countries. Many receive no help other than that provided by families and friends (ie little or no medical care; no state benefits; no community support). Most have no chance of employment – as a result, some end up begging on the streets in order to survive.

Who are the disabled?

'Disability' is a very general term. People described as 'disabled' include:

- the mentally handicapped (see **A**);
- the physically handicapped. This includes people born with a physical defect or people suffering from crippling diseases such as muscular dystrophy or multiple sclerosis;
- people who have suffered a serious accident or illness, with long-term or permanent effects;
- the blind and the deaf.

The severity of the disability is also important. Many people with minor disabilities are able to lead completely normal lives. For the severely handicapped, however, it may be difficult to do the simplest things without help.

The International Year of the Disabled

In 1971 the United Nations (see Unit 9.2) set out the rights of mentally handicapped people. In 1975 they did the same for the physically handicapped. 1981 was the Year of the Disabled. The United Nations gave it the motto:

Full participation and equality

and set out five objectives it hoped the year would achieve:

1 To help disabled people become physically and mentally adjusted to life in their community;
2 To support all national and international efforts to train and educate disabled people to live as full a life as possible. All disabled people have a right to expect to work and to be fully integrated into society.

3 To encourage shops and public places to make access for disabled people easier.
4 To educate the general public about the rights and needs of disabled people.
5 To prevent as much disability as possible and to help in the rehabilitation of disabled people.

---

3 What do you think the UN meant by the motto; 'Full participation and equality'?
4 Choose one of the five objectives of the Year of the Disabled.
  a) Explain in your own words what it means.
  b) State how far you think it has been achieved, and what more could be done.

A   *Professor Stephen Hawking*
Stephen Hawking is totally crippled by a form of sclerosis. He has gained a worldwide reputation as a mathematical genius, particularly for his research into the origins of the Universe.

Who helps?

Many societies and groups work to serve the needs of the disabled, in the UK and worldwide. One of these is the Spastics Society. This charity was set up in 1952. It has five objectives:

1 To provide and promote facilities for the treatment, training, education and residential care of men, women and children with cerebral palsy.
2 To foster understanding of cerebral palsy and help people to accept it.
3 To provide help and support for disabled people and their families.
4 To promote research into the causes, treatment and prevention of cerebral palsy.
5 To show how authorities at all levels can and should help people with cerebral palsy.

---

5 Try to find out more about cerebral palsy and the work of the Spastics Society.
6 Do you think society does enough to meet the needs of the disabled? What more could be done?

By way of definition

- A *disabled person* is someone who, because of their mental or physical disabilities, needs special help.
- Someone suffering from *cerebral palsy* has difficulty in controlling their speech and movements. The areas of the brain which affect these functions may not have developed properly, or may have been damaged at birth.
- *Spasticity* is a particular kind of cerebral palsy.

A matter of opinion

I can't help feeling embarrassed when I meet handicapped people. I never know whether to say anything about their disability or ignore it altogether. So I find it difficult to talk naturally with them.

People assume that just because I'm in a wheelchair I can't think independently. Sometimes they ask my Mum how I'm feeling – as if I can't talk for myself! Why can't they accept me as a person?

I belong to a club for both physically-handicapped and able-bodied people. We have a great time. It's taught me a lot about the needs of disabled people.

- Choose one of these statements and explain how it makes you feel.

5.3 Abortion – the facts

People talk as if abortion is an easy way out. They can have no idea of the mental agony I went through. I'll never know if it was the right decision. I was very young and very confused. My family and friends all said I'd be a fool to saddle myself with a kid, and my boyfriend didn't want to know. I still think a lot about my baby, you know, and wonder what he would have been like ...

Karen, 22

Before 1967 abortion was against the law in Britain. Yet thousands of illegal 'back street' abortions were performed each year – often in horrific conditions. Women who had an abortion did not only break the law – they risked death or serious injury if anything went wrong.

The Abortion Act of 1967 was intended to put an end to this situation. It made abortion legal in certain circumstances:

- It must be carried out before the time of 'viability' – that is before the foetus is capable of surviving without its mother. Medical opinion is that a baby may be able to survive after 28 weeks.
- Two registered medical practitioners (doctors) must agree that the abortion is permissible under law.
- The doctors must agree that to continue the pregnancy would involve a risk to the life of the pregnant mother, or an injury to the physical or mental health of the woman or existing children in the family.
  OR They must agree that there is a substantial risk that, if born, the baby would be severely mentally or physically handicapped.

There is great controversy over abortion. Many people welcomed the 1967 Act, and some feel that it did not go far enough towards allowing women to choose whether or not to have an abortion. Others, however, are violently opposed to abortion, and feel that the clauses of the Act are too general, allowing women to obtain abortion 'on demand'.

1 Read through the conditions of the 1967 Act again.
a) Do you think they are strict? Or do you think they could be interpreted in different ways?
b) What situation did the Act try to end?

Stages in development

The limit of 28 weeks was chosen because at that point a baby has some chance of surviving on its own. But is that the point at which the foetus becomes a human being? **A** shows the stages in the development of a foetus in the womb.

- At 17 days the foetus grows its own blood cells.
- At 24 days the heart develops.
- After six weeks the skeleton has formed, the foetus has reflexes and wave patterns can be recorded in the brain.
- At eight weeks the brain, liver, kidneys and stomach function.
- At 16 weeks the sexual organs and vocal chords have formed.

Thanks to modern technology, a premature baby born after only 25 weeks of pregnancy still has a good chance of survival.

2 At what stage do you think the foetus becomes a human being: When it is conceived? When its brain develops? When it could survive without its mother? When it is born? Give reasons for your answer
3 Does your answer to question 2 affect your view on abortion? In what way?
4 Some people argue that abortion after 18 weeks should be illegal. What do you think?
5 Do you think abortion is too easy, or not easy enough? Explain your answer.

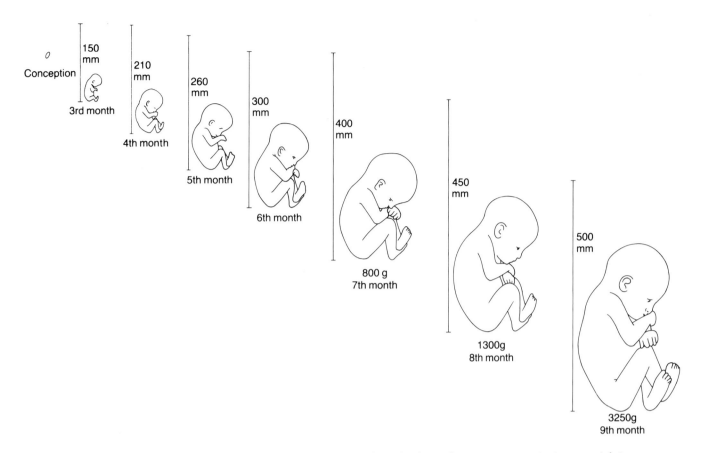

A *Stages in the growth of the embryo and foetus. At what stage does the foetus become a person in its own right?*

B Abortion – the facts

- Before 1967 an estimated 200,000 back-street abortions were performed each year in Britain. Around 60 women a year died as a result.
- In 1986 157,000 legal abortions were carried out in this country – that's about 300 a day. Around 20% of abortions are performed on women from other countries – especially Spain and Southern Ireland, where abortion is illegal.
- Although the legal limit on abortion is 28 weeks, in practice it is rarely performed after 22 weeks. Only urgent medical reasons are usually accepted as justification for abortion after this.
- A GP who has 2500 patients will probably receive about 10 requests for abortions each year.
- About 18% of all babies conceived are aborted.

6 Do you find any of the statistics in **B** surprising or shocking? Which ones, and why?

By way of definition

- *abortion* – operation to stop a pregnancy, usually performed before 28 weeks.

A matter of opinion

Abortion kills babies. (Anti-abortion poster)

The right of personal privacy includes the abortion decision. Ruling of US Supreme Court.

A woman has the right to choose. (Feminist slogan)

- Which of these statements do you agree with, and why?

MATTERS OF LIFE AND DEATH

5.4 Abortion – the issues

Abortion is murder. From the moment of conception a baby is a person. It doesn't matter whether it's one day old or nine months old. All these arguments about 18 weeks or 22 weeks are just avoiding the issue.

Asif, 18

As we saw in Unit 5.3, abortion is a highly controversial issue. What do the two 'sides' in the controversy have to say?

Abortion should be legally available to all women

The movement to legalise abortion started in the 1930s. The Abortion Law Reform Society was set up in 1936. Some members of the medical profession and members of the Women's Movement are in favour of a further relaxation of the laws. Some Christians accept that abortion, although always regrettable, may be necessary in certain situations.

A *Members of the anti-abortion movement LIFE campaign to save the unborn child.*

52

Pro-abortionists argue that:

1 Every woman has the right to decide what happens to her body. It is the woman who must have the last word on whether or not to bear a child.
2 Every baby has the right to be born into a family which will provide the basic necessities of life: shelter, food, clothing etc. If this basic care is not guaranteed, then an abortion is justified.
3 There are too many unwanted children in the world – why add more?
4 Other members of the family also have rights. This includes the woman's parents (if she is unmarried) since they may well have to look after her and the baby. If a married woman wants an abortion, it is important to consider the needs of her husband and other children.
5 If a woman discovers that her child will be severely handicapped, she must be allowed to decide whether she can cope with looking after that child.
6 A woman who becomes pregnant after being raped should not be expected to carry the child of the man who assaulted her.
7 Sometimes abortion is not the easy way out; it requires a mature, responsible decision.

Abortion should not be allowed

The Society for the Protection of the Unborn Child (SPUC) is strongly opposed to abortion (A). Many members are Roman Catholics, who believe that abortion is totally wrong. So do Christians of many other denominations.

The 'anti-abortionists' argue that:

1 Every child is a precious and unique gift from God. We have no right to destroy that gift under any circumstances whatsoever (this would even include the case of a woman who had been raped).
2 A defenceless baby needs special protection, since it cannot argue for its own rights. The rights of the unborn child are at least equal to those of the pregnant mother.
3 The foetus is a human being from the moment of conception since, if left alone, it will continue to develop as a person.
4 A person who is physically or mentally handicapped can nevertheless lead a full and rewarding life – and give love and joy to family and friends.

5 If people were more educated, and more responsible, about contraception, there would be fewer unwanted pregnancies and therefore no need for abortion. (Catholics, of course, would not support this argument – see Unit 2.8.)
6 Abortion places a heavy burden on doctors and nurses who have to carry it out. For some, it may be asking them to commit murder.

---

1 Which of the arguments *in favour* of abortion do you find most convincing, and why?
2 Which of the arguments *against* abortion do you find most convincing, and why?
3 Overall, which group do you think has the strongest case – the pro-abortion campaigners or the anti-abortion campaigners?
4 Which side do *you* support, and why?
5 A lot is said about the woman's right to choose. Do you think anyone else has a right to be involved in the decision – eg the baby's father, the woman's family?

A Christian viewpoint?

The majority of Christians are deeply unhappy about both abortion and the problem of unwanted pregnancies. The church teaches that people should have a responsible attitude towards sex (see Unit 2.3). Most Christians feel that the best way in which a couple can express their commitment to one another is in marriage – any child they then have is a gift from God.

A matter of opinion

In 1974 the Medical Defence Union issued this statement about abortion:

When the girl is under 16 her parents always should be consulted unless she forbids the practitioner to do so. The written consent of the parents should be obtained but their refusal should not be allowed to prevent a lawful termination to which the patient herself consents and which is considered to be clinically necessary. Conversely a termination should never be carried out in opposition to a girl's wishes even if the parents demand it.

● Do you think that a girl under 16 should be able to obtain an abortion without her parents' consent?
● In what circumstances might a girl's parents want her to have an abortion?

5.5 Euthanasia

I can't bear the thought of lingering on – probably in a lot of pain – and being a burden to everyone. Surely people have a right to die in a dignified way, and to choose when? Mind you, it's easy to say that now, when I'm young and fit. Perhaps I'll see things differently when I'm old.

Sara, 17

The subject of *euthanasia* (choosing to die – or not to prolong life) causes controversy whenever it is mentioned. Some people argue that everyone has the right to an easy, dignified death. Others maintain that life must be preserved at all costs, and that euthanasia is no different from murder. Many would adopt a middle view – feeling that in some circumstances, euthanasia is permissible.

Involuntary euthanasia

Euthanasia is illegal in Britain and many other countries. But in some cases a person may be 'allowed to die' when prolonging their life can only lead to more suffering – and costly treatment. Examples might be:

- when a person is 'clinically dead' (sometimes referred to as 'brain dead') but is connected to a life-support machine which continues to operate the heart and lungs. There is no possibility that the person will recover, and with the agreement of the family a doctor may decide to switch off the machine.
- a baby born with such serious deformities that its quality of life will be very poor. If the parents agree, doctors may decide not to try to prolong the baby's life.
- an old person with a disease that can be treated – but only by taking action that would give rise to another incurable condition. Doctors may decide to do nothing.

In each of these cases, the patient is allowed to die. The doctors decide *not* to do something that will keep the person alive. But the patient him or herself is unable to give their consent. The final decision is taken by a doctor, in consultation with relatives. Such decisions are almost always made on grounds of compassion, to avoid further suffering. Opponents of euthanasia argue that unscrupulous relatives might persuade a doctor to stop treatment, or that hard-pressed medical staff might consider the cost of further treatment rather than the needs of the patient.

---

1 Would you be happy for someone to take a life-or-death decision on your behalf?

Throughout history there have been horrifying examples of *compulsory* euthanasia. During the Second World War, for example, the Nazis set out to eliminate everyone who was physically or mentally handicapped, on the grounds that this would help stamp out hereditary diseases and disabilities.

A *A motorist is critically injured in a car crash. Who decides whether she should live or die?*

Voluntary euthanasia

Many people accept that when someone is terminally ill, or on a life-support system, life and death decisions may have to be taken. But the debate becomes particularly heated over *voluntary* euthanasia, when a person chooses when and how to die.

The pros and cons

Those in favour of euthanasia – such as members of the society called EXIT – argue that:

1 Everyone has the right to die with dignity and to choose when and how they will die.
2 Everyone has the right to choose an easy death – release from a painful, useless existence.
3 A speedy and peaceful death spares relatives and friends the pain of watching a loved one suffer.
4 Costly medical resources used to prolong life could be devoted to those who can be cured.

Those against euthanasia say that:

1 There are ways in which people can die with dignity – for example, in a Hospice (see Unit 5.6).
2 Human beings are not the same as animals – they can't be 'put to sleep'.
3 Only God has the right to decide when a person should die.
4 Doctors are bound by the 'Hippocratic Oath' which says they must save life at all costs.
5 A person who is suffering may not be capable of making a rational decision
6 People sometimes recover against all the odds.
7 It is unfair to place the burden of administering euthanasia on to medical staff or relations.

---

2 a) Which do you think is the best argument in favour of euthanasia?
b) Which do you think is the best argument against euthanasia?
c) Which side do you support, and why?

In the Netherlands, euthanasia is technically illegal, but doctors can administer it without fear of prosecution, as long as they follow a detailed set of guidelines. The doctor must be able to prove:

- that he or she followed the wishes of the patient – whose request for euthanasia was made voluntarily;
- that he or she outlined fully the alternatives available;
- that a colleague was brought in for a second opinion.

Death is usually by fatal injection or tablets. The doctor's file is passed on to the police or the coroner, who may investigate further if there are any doubts about the case.

An estimated 10,000 Dutch people choose euthanasia each year – that's about 8% of all deaths. And about 70% of Dutch people believe that euthanasia should be available as an option.

---

3 Members of EXIT and other supporters of euthanasia would like to follow the Dutch example. What do you think?

The Christian view

The Roman Catholic Church is totally opposed to all forms of euthanasia. Catholics argue that life is a precious gift from God, and only God can take it away. Many Christians from other denominations share this view. Some churches, however, are not opposed to euthanasia in principle, as long as strict safeguards are applied.

A matter of opinion

Anything which says to the very ill or the very old that there is no longer anything that matters in their life would be a deep impoverishment to the whole of society.

Dr Ciceley Saunders, founder of the Hospice Movement

Some old people feel that they are a burden to their family, and that they would be better off dead ... What sort of society could let its old folk die because they are 'in the way'?

A doctor specialising in the care of elderly patients

- Do you agree or disagree? Give reasons for your answer

5.6 The Hospice Movement

My Gran died last year – in a hospice. I was quite scared the first time I went to visit her there. I expected it to be really depressing. But it was quite different. The staff were relaxed and cheerful, and the patients could do what they liked. They even let us take Gran's dog in! Gran knew she was dying, but she was quite calm about it. She said she was glad not to be a burden on anyone.

Katy, 14

The first hospice was set up by Irish nuns – the Sisters of Charity – in Dublin, towards the end of the nineteenth century. In 1900 five of the sisters travelled to England, to the East End of London, where they carried on their work of caring for the dying. Within a few years they had established St Joseph's Hospice.

Almost 60 years later a young nurse called Ciceley Saunders went to work at St Joseph's. Although her nursing career was cut short by illness, she went on to establish many other hospices, starting with St Christopher's, which was opened in 1969.

Now there are almost 100 in-patient hospice units around the country. At any one time, they provide care for about 2000 patients – young and old, men and women. Most of the units are run by charities, and many have a Christian basis, although the patients need not be Christian.

Hospices operate all over the world. Perhaps the most famous is the one set up by Mother Teresa of Calcutta, to care for the poor of that city.

Aims of the hospice movement

Hospices share the same objective: to offer care and support for people who are dying, and their families. This objective covers three main aims:

1 To relieve pain – whether it is caused by the illness itself, or by the stress and fear it creates.
2 To enable patients and their families to face up to death – to talk about their fears and distress in a relaxed, open atmosphere.

3 To care for the emotional needs of relatives – before, during and after the patient's death.

---

1 People rarely talk about death in our society – it is a 'taboo' subject. Do you think the hospice approach would help people come to terms with death?

How hospices help

Most hospices offer fairly short-term care. Patients rarely stay longer than six months. Some come only for a week or two, to give relatives a chance for a rest or a holiday. Often a person will spend some time in a hospice and then return home for a while. This is an important part of the hospice philosophy. It leaves the patient with a sense of independence and enables them to develop a real relationship with the hospice staff, while coming to terms with the idea of death.

Hospice staff are trained in providing for the needs of the dying person's relatives. For example, the family may feel guilty because they have been unable to look after a loved one at home; or parents may need the freedom to grieve in their own way for a dead child.

Some hospices are devoted to the care of children and young people. One of these is Helen House in Oxford. Its Director, Mother Frances Dominica, explains how she sees the role of the hospice:

A *(it) is to be alongside the family offering friendship, support and practical help; it can be seen as an artificial extended family ... the members of the hospice team are fellow human beings whose task it is to support the members of the family in their role, not to take over as the experts; to enable and enhance the skills and expertise of the family; and to share in the care of the child and the family as and when they are invited to do so. The aim of the children's hospice should be to make it possible for a family to care for their sick child at home most of the time by:*

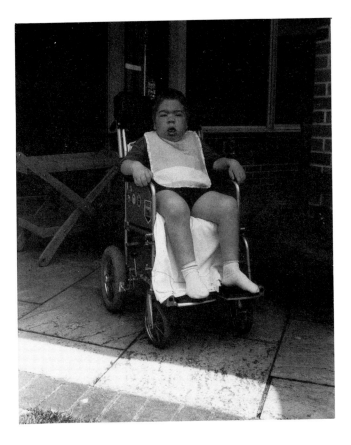

B *A stay in a hospice gives the parents of terminally-ill children a chance for a holiday or a rest from fulltime care.*

care is taken to cater for each individual's needs – whether it is a new hair-do, seeing a loved pet, shopping expeditions, games or music.

Many hospices are run by Christian charities, and the staff themselves may be Christian – although patients do not have to have any religious beliefs.

- *Ensuring that available community services are mobilized where appropriate.*
- *Offering occasional respite care for the child with or without other members of the family, as they choose.*
- *Telephone contact and home visits.*
- *Offering support and help in the place of the family's choosing during the terminal phase and giving advice about funeral arrangements if asked to do so.*
- *Continuing to provide support following the death of the child.*

---

2 List what you think are the three most important features of hospice care. Explain why you chose them.

What are hospices like?

No two hospices are the same. Some are very small, with a homely atmosphere. Others are much larger. But all provide continual love and support. Great

A matter of opinion

A children's hospice is not, in the vast majority of cases, a place where children are taken to die. The definition of the word hospice is 'a place of shelter for pilgrims and travellers'. In its modern form, hospice still offers hospitality to those on a journey, the journey from this life to the next ... by giving them permission to be who they are and ensuring that they are in a loving, supportive environment, it is possible to help them to meet death with a dignity and a nobility which in no way denies grief.
Mother Frances Dominica, Director, Helen House

Hospices aim to create an atmosphere of openness and trust, where emotional and spiritual pain can be honestly faced and relieved, along with physical pain. They treat the dying with dignity and respond to needs as patients perceive them.
Denise Winn *The Hospice Way*

Accepting death's coming is the very opposite of doing nothing. Dame Cicely Saunders

- Why do you think 'dying with dignity' is so important to people? Explain briefly, in your own words, how hospices aim to achieve this objective.
- Do you find Cicely Saunders' comment surprising? What do you think she meant? Do you agree?

MATTERS OF LIFE AND DEATH

5.7 Suicide

Everything seemed to be falling apart ... I'd just broken up with my boyfriend, there was a lot of pressure at work and rows at home. I simply couldn't cope. There didn't seem to be any point in living. I can remember taking the sleeping tablets and thinking 'Now I can sleep for ever ...'

Kim, 23

A Suicide – the facts

1 Until 1961 suicide was illegal in Great Britain. Someone who tried – and failed – could well face prosecution. Suicide itself is no longer against the law, but anyone who assists another person in a suicide attempt is breaking the law.
2 Every day about 1200 people in the world commit suicide. In the UK, about 15 people kill themselves each day.
3 Women are more likely to attempt suicide than men.
4 The most vulnerable age group is between 20 and 45.
5 About 1 in 10 of those who fail in one suicide bid later take their own lives.

1 Why do you think that women are more likely than men to attempt suicide?
2 Why do you think it is illegal to help someone else commit suicide?

A way of escape?

To someone as desperate as Kim, suicide can appear to be the only escape from their problems. It is impossible to pinpoint exactly what leads a person to think of killing themselves – or what tips the balance in turning thought into action. A whole range of complex factors are usually involved. Some of the most common problems are:

- personal worries: loneliness, financial difficulties, fear of redundancy, anxiety about old age;
- depression or serious illness;
- mental instability;
- alcohol or drug abuse;
- social pressures: guilt about past actions; work pressures; examinations; bullying or victimisation.

These and many other pressures may build up until a person feels that he or she simply 'can't cope' any longer.

A cry for help?

You may have heard a suicide attempt described as 'a cry for help'. It was to answer such cries that the Reverend Chad Varah set up the Samaritans.

In 1953 Chad Varah was a Church of England priest, working in London. He was appalled at the number of suicide attempts he heard about. So he installed a telephone in his church vestry. Word soon spread that if anyone was feeling desperate or contemplating suicide they could ring Chad Varah to talk about their problems.

Today there are over 180 branches of the Samaritans in Britain, staffed by about 20,000 volunteers. The telephones are manned 24 hours a day, 365 days a year – so there is always someone to listen and, perhaps, offer advice. The Samaritans receive more than 300,000 telephone calls a year.

Being a Samaritan is not easy. Each volunteer is interviewed. If accepted, the volunteer has a period of training, and is then expected to do a regular 3–4 hour shift each week (including some overnight work). Perhaps one of the hardest things for a volunteer to accept is that they are usually only a voice at the end of the telephone (**B**):

B *'Volunteers have to resist their natural impulse to solve some desperate cases by giving material comfort ... They have to accept that a client's sworn promise to phone next day is often not kept ... they have to accept that gratitude doesn't necessarily follow weeks and months of time spent*

58

on cases ... that often the person helped doesn't even remember his name. The volunteer discovers that he is what he actually chooses to be – faceless, nameless, just a voice or an ear and nothing more.'
'One of the hardest things is simply not knowing what happens after you put down the phone ...'

---

3 Look up the parable of the Good Samaritan (Luke 10, 30–37). Why do you think Chad Varah chose this name for his telephone help-line?
4 What qualities do you think a good modern Samaritan should possess?

The Christian attitude towards suicide

Most Christians believe that life is a sacred gift from God. It follows that only God can take this gift away. A person who tries to take his or her own life, then, is 'playing at God'.

In the past most Christian churches were very strict about suicide. They taught that a person who killed himself committed a grave sin and would go to hell. Suicide victims were not buried in the consecrated (holy) ground of the churchyard, but outside the churchyard wall. This was hard on the person's family and friends, who felt very ashamed.

Nowadays, attitudes are changing. Most Christian churches seek to understand the pressures that may lead someone to take their own life, and many attempt to provide care and counselling for those who feel desperate.

---

5 Why do you think Christian attitudes towards suicide are changing? Do you think this is right, or should the church maintain its strict position?
6 Do you think a person has the right to take their own life? Explain your answer.

A matter of opinion

People who commit suicide are cowards. They take the easy way out, without thinking about their families and friends.

● Do you agree? Say why/why not.

5.8 Science and life: the 'biotechnological revolution'

We had been trying for six years to have a baby. Eventually the doctor suggested artificial insemination. I rejected the idea at first, because it seemed so unnatural. But Geoff, my husband, was keen, so we went ahead. I'm expecting our baby in the autumn. It's like a dream come true.

Sheila, 31

We hear a lot about the number of abortions, the problem of teenage pregnancy and unwanted babies. But there is much less news coverage of another major problem: infertility. 10% of couples in Britain are childless. For some, this is a deliberate choice. Many others long for a baby but – for one of many possible reasons – are unable to conceive. Infertility affects both men and women; it can be a heartbreaking problem.

In the past, there was little a couple could do. They simply had to accept that it was 'the will of God' that they should not have children. Some might adopt or foster a child. Today, however, medical science has opened up various possibilities. There are three main options – each of which raises complex, controversial issues.

1 AIH – artificial insemination of the woman, using her husband's semen. This method can be used where a husband is healthy and tests show that he can father a child, but his wife has a physical condition such as blocked Fallopian tubes, which prevents her becoming pregnant. Sperms are taken from the husband and implanted surgically in the wife's body.

Those opposed to any form of artificial insemination argue that it is unnatural and against the will of God. Most people, however, see AIH as simply a means of medicine giving husband and wife a helping hand.

---

1 Do you think that it is 'wrong' or 'unnatural' for medicine to intervene in this way? Present arguments for and against AIH.

---

2 AID – artificial insemination of the woman using an unknown donor's sperm. AID is a possibility for couples where the wife is able to conceive but tests reveal that her husband is infertile – for example, his sperm count may be very low, or his sperms inactive. Sperms from an unknown donor are implanted in the woman.

This raises far more controversial questions:

- Is AID a form of adultery, as many Christians maintain?
- Is the child genuinely the product of the husband and wife?
- Husband and wife may agree to AID – but what happens if the husband later rejects 'another man's child'?
- If a couple desperately want a child, does it really matter how it is conceived?
- Will AID lead on to 'genetic engineering' – ie where a woman selects sperm from a particular type of donor (eg a top sportsman) in the hopes that her child will inherit these characteristics? Some experiments have already taken place in the United States, with women selecting sperm from a bank of highly-intelligent donors.

---

2 Would you be happy to use AID, if there was no alternative?

---

3 IVF (in vitro fertilisation). This involves removing an egg from the woman, fertilising it – with her husband's semen – in a laboratory, then replacing the fertilised egg in the woman's body to develop as a normal foetus. In 1978 Louise Brown, the world's first 'test-tube' baby, was born. Since then over 200 babies have been conceived in this way. Once again, IVF raises many controversial questions:

- As long as the wife's egg and the husband's sperm are used, does it make any difference that conception occurs outside the body?
- Is this taking 'unnatural' methods of fertilisation too far?
- What if the wife's egg is fertilised by a donor's sperm?

---

3 Imagine you were to discover that you had been conceived by in vitro fertilisation. Would it make a great difference to you? In what ways?

A further complication arises in the case of so-called 'surrogate' motherhood. This is when a husband and wife donate egg and sperm for in vitro fertilisation – but the fertilised egg is then placed in another woman's body and *she* goes through the pregnancy and delivery, before returning the child to its natural parents. What kinds of issues might this raise?

Alternatively, a couple may ask (or pay) another woman to be fertilised by the husband's sperm and carry the baby until it is born. Is this 'adultery by consent'?

In 1984 the Warnock Committee was set up to look into some of these controversial issues. It recommended that:

- it is natural to try to cure infertility;
- there are no serious objections to AIH;
- AID is not the same as adultery since it is done with the husband's consent.

A matter of opinion

Infertility causes great sorrow and distress for many couples. But, from the medical point of view, treatment costs a great deal in terms of time and resources. A hospital gynaecologist commented:

... I spend a lot of my time talking to infertile couples and I realise the anguish that they are going through. But I sometimes feel that this form of treatment takes up a disproportionate amount of time, effort and resources – which could be used to save lives, rather than create them ...

- Do you think the time, effort and resources used in infertility treatment and research could be better used in other ways? Give your reasons.

60

6.1 The law – and breaking it

Of course we need laws in this country. Without laws everyone would be free to do what they liked – and that would be total anarchy. But I sometimes wonder if we're surrounded by too many laws nowadays. It's quite difficult not to break the law sometimes. I'm not a criminal, but I do sometimes break the speed limit ... If we're going to get really technical, I suppose taking home a few pens from the office is 'theft' – but where do you draw the line?

Mark, 19

Are we becoming increasingly bound by laws and restrictions? As life becomes more complicated, we seem to need more laws to control it. Think, for example, of the changes in the laws that apply to cars and driving. Less than 60 years ago, you didn't even need to take a driving test – can you imagine what would happen if that was still the case?

---

1 Can you imagine life in a society which had no laws? To help you, think about your class at school. If there were no rules, who would gain power, and how? Who would suffer? What would *you* do?

What is the law?

As you can see from the motoring example, laws must change in order to keep up with developments in society. Changes in the law may also reflect alterations in people's attitudes. For example, in the last 30 years Parliament has passed laws legalising abortion and homosexuality (see Units 2.9 and 5.3).

What is against 'the law' in one country or culture may be quite permissible in another. In Britain, for example, it is illegal for a man to have more than one wife (if a man does have two wives, he can be prosecuted for being a bigamist). But in Muslim countries the law permits a man to have more than one wife (but not vice versa) since this is permitted by the Qur'an or Muslim scriptures. However, the Qur'an forbids Muslims to take alcohol, and possession of alcohol is banned in Muslim countries. This is certainly not the case in Britain!

Almost all countries and societies, however, outlaw criminal activities such as murder, rape and robbery, although they vary in the way these crimes are punished.

---

2 Do you think that life in Britain is restricted by too many laws? Or do you think that we need more laws, not less? Give reasons for your answer.
3 Can you think of one law that you would like to change? What, how, and why?

Crime

There are two types of crime:

1 *Indictable offences* – these are the most serious kinds of crime, including murder, manslaughter, rape and other acts of violence. Someone accused of an indictable offence is usually tried before a judge and jury and, if convicted, may face imprisonment or a heavy fine.
2 *Non-indictable offences* – these are less serious offences, such as motoring offences, petty theft, damage to property. They are usually tried before a magistrate in a local court. If found guilty a person is usually fined or put on probation, rather than being sent to prison – unless the crime was particularly serious or the person had committed many previous offences.

Of course, it is impossible to know how often the law is broken in this country. Most 'crimes' go undetected and unreported. However, offences reported to the police *are* recorded. **A** shows the numbers of offences recorded by the police in 1971 and 1986.

A Crime in the UK

	Cases recorded in UK (thousands)	
Type of crime	1971	1986
Violence against the person	53.4	141.3
Sexual offences	26.4	26.2
Burglary	521.3	1048.5
Robbery	10.4	36.3
Drugs offences	...	12.9
Theft and handling stolen goods	1116.9	2247.5
Fraud and forgery	110.7	168.2
Criminal damage	56.4	666.6
Other	11.1	32.1
Total	1906.6	4379.6

3 Look at **A**. Which types of crimes have increased most dramatically since 1971? Why do you think this is?

4 Try to suggest two reasons for each of the findings in **B**.

B Crime – the facts

1 In 1951 638,000 offences were reported. Today around 4,000,000 crimes are reported each year;

2 Men are seven times more likely than women to commit crime;

3 Most crimes are committed by people under the age of 25 – particularly by those between the ages of 16 and 19;

4 The crime rate in towns and cities is much higher than in country areas.

Why do people break the law?

There are many views on what leads people to crime:

- Some people might reply that it's human nature! Most of us dislike being told what to do and what not to do. It's only natural that, like children, we are 'naughty' from time to time.

- Some Christians believe that the Devil, or our own evil nature, constantly leads us into temptation. Only God can save us from sin/breaking the law. The increasing amount of crime reflects a breakdown in society's religious and moral standards.

- Sociologists argue that home background and the stresses of modern life are to blame – young people are easily led by the rest of the gang;

unemployment and boredom may lead them to seek the excitement of drugs, muggings and violence.

- Greed is often blamed. We are surrounded by advertisements that lead us to want more and more material goods. We may resent what our neighbours possess – and in some cases this may lead us to steal it.

- Some criticise the police for poor detection rates. Only about 1 in 7 crimes is solved. This leads criminals to feel that they can get away with it.

5 Which of these reasons do *you* think is the main cause of crime? Can you add any others to the list?

What does the Bible say?

Christian views on right and wrong are based, in part, on the 'Ten Commandments':

Exodus 20.3–17
1 *You shall have no other gods before me.*
2 *You shall not make for yourself a graven image, or any likeness ... you shall not bow down to them or serve them ...*
3 *You shall not take the name of the Lord your God in vain ...*
4 *Remember the sabbath day, to keep it holy. Six days you shall labour, and do all your work; the seventh day is a sabbath to the Lord your God ...*
5 *Honour your father and your mother ...*
6 *You shall not kill.*
7 *You shall not commit adultery.*
8 *You shall not steal.*
9 *You shall not bear false witness against your neighbour.*
10 *You shall not covet ...*

- Do you think the ten commandments still apply in the modern world?
- Write your own list of commandments for today.

A matter of opinion

Young people are not totally responsible for their criminal behaviour. Society must take a lot of the blame.

- Do you agree? Or do you think that this is just evading the issue?

6.2 Punishment

Shutting a person up in prison doesn't achieve any-thing ... It certainly doesn't turn them into a re-formed character. In fact, they probably meet even worse criminals and become hardened ... I think it is better to make them do something to help their victims – you know, a mugger doing gardening for old people ... that sort of thing.

Najma, 15

Prisons are too soft these days. What criminals need is a hard lesson, not colour TV and basket-work! And a 'life' sentence should mean life.

Gary, 15

Najma and Gary have very different views about how prisoners should be treated. Most of us learn at a very early age that we will be punished when we do something wrong. You can probably remem-ber times when you were sent to bed early, or didn't get any pocket money, because you had committed some minor 'crime'.

What is the point of punishment? What form should that punishment take? These issues are the subject of considerable debate.

Crime and punishment

If someone is found guilty of breaking the law, they will be punished. For minor offences, they may have to pay a fine, or serve a period on probation. For more serious crimes, they may be sent to prison (in this country) – or even sentenced to death (in countries which have not abolished capital punish-ment). A person is usually punished for four reasons:

1 *Retribution* – making the person pay for what he or she has done. You've probably heard people say 'We should give the thugs and hooligans a taste of their own medicine'. Sometimes this view is taken to extremes. A judge in South Carolina offered a rapist the choice between castration and

going to prison. Writing about this, the *New York Times* asked:

'Why not offer pickpockets the choice between prison and amputation or threaten 'Peeping Toms' with blindness?'

Some countries have much harsher punishments than others. Many still have the death penalty for very serious crimes (see Unit 6.4), and in certain Muslim countries a thief might have his or her hand cut off for theft or robbery in accordance with the teaching of the Qur'an.

---

1 Have you ever felt that you wanted to get your own back on someone who had hurt you? What did you do? Do you think this is the right way for society to treat criminals? Who gains?

---

2 *Protection* for other members of society. Shut-ting a criminal away means that they cannot en-danger other people or their property. They can be prevented from breaking the law at least for a time.

---

2 Can you think of any flaws in the argument that says criminals should be locked away to protect society?

---

3 *Deterrence* – to put offenders off committing any further crimes, and to make an example of them so that other people find crime less attractive. Those in favour of harsher penalties often argue that they are effective deterrents. But in practice this rarely works. Over 75% of people who have been in prison return again (they are called 'recidiv-ists').

---

3 Why do you think imprisonment does not seem to work as a deterrent? Do you think that harsher penalties would be more effective in putting people off crime?

---

4 *Reform* – to change the criminal and his or her attitudes, so that they no longer want to commit crimes. This is particularly important for young offenders, who have their whole lives ahead of them. An effective programme of reform could mean that a young delinquent stays clear of trouble for the rest of his or her life. Around 160,000 young people (under the age of 17) go through the courts each year. If convicted, there are a variety of options available to deal with them (see below) – most of which aim to reform as well as punish. It is much more difficult to establish any real reform programme for adults. Around 42,000 men are in prison at any given time – but Britain's prisons were only built to take around 25,000 prisoners. Overcrowding and shortages of staff mean that there can be very little 'reforming'. **A** is a work-room inside a British prison.

---

4 Do you think more emphasis on reform would help cut down the crime rate? Or is this just being 'soft' on criminals?

Forms of punishment

When a criminal is found guilty the court must then decide on the most appropriate form of punishment. This will depend on a great many factors including the seriousness of the crime, the criminal's age, background and circumstances, and any previous criminal record. A number of options are available:

- A fine – to be paid to the court either as a lump sum or as a series of regular instalments.
- Probation – the offender has to make regular contact with a probation officer for a set period, and must not leave the area without first notifying the probation officer.
- Attendance centre – juveniles and young offenders may be ordered to attend an Attendance Centre for sessions of around 2 hours, until they have 'paid off' a period of, say, 12 or 24 hours.
- Binding over – the offender pays a sum of money to the court as a sort of 'guarantee' that they will not break the law again within a set period of time. If they do commit another offence, they lose the money.

A *A prison work room. Do you think conditions like these are too comfortable for offenders?*

- Community Service Order – this orders an offender to work on some community scheme or project (eg a play scheme or old people's centre) for a length of time – from 40 to 240 hours. The work is unpaid and the sentence must be completed within 12 months.
- Day Training Centre – young offenders attend day centres to receive training for a future career. The attendance may be for up to 60 days.
- Detention Centre – male offenders between 15 and 20 may be held in detention for up to four months.
- Imprisonment – an offender may be sent to prison for any term up to life (for very serious crimes).

What does the Bible say?

Leviticus 24.17–20
He who kills a man shall be put to death. He who kills a beast shall make it good, life for life. When a man causes a disfigurement in his neighbour, as he has done it shall be done to him, fracture for fracture, eye for eye, tooth for tooth; as he has disfigured a man, he shall be disfigured.

Matthew 5. 38–39
'You have heard that it was said, "An eye for an eye and a tooth for a tooth." But I say to you, "Do not resist one who is evil. But if any one strikes you on the right cheek, turn to him the other also.'

The first extract is from the Old Testament, the second gives the words of Jesus in the New Testament.

- What is the Christian view of punishment?

A matter of opinion

To punish is to injure; to reform is to heal. You cannot mend a person by damaging him.
George Bernard Shaw

Of course we should spend time trying to make the prisoner see sense – but you try doing that with prisoners living three to a cell and cooped up for 23 hours a day.

Prison officer

Although we recognise that there is little evidence for the success of attempts to make prison a place of rehabilitation, we believe that it is still our Christian duty to attempt to make it so.
Member of a Christian working party

- Choose one of these extracts and explain what you think the speaker means. Do you agree or disagree? What could be done to improve the situation?

6.3 Non-violent protest

In our RE lesson we were talking about 'turning the other cheek'. It sounded really weak at first. But then when I thought about it, it's really a hard thing to do. Sometimes violence seems to be a natural reaction. But I don't think it's a good way of solving problems.

Pam, 14

If you watch children squabbling in the playground – or adults on the football pitch – it is easy to see how quickly a minor dispute can explode into anger and violence. Sometimes a peaceful demonstration like the Soweto March (see Unit 4.4) or the rally of Chinese students in May 1989 ends in terror and tragedy.

In this century two outstanding figures have denounced violence and spoken out for a new form of non-violent protest: *passive resistance*. They were Mahatma Gandhi and Martin Luther King. Both men put their ideas into action – and both, sadly, met violent deaths.

Mahatma Gandhi (1869–1948)

Gandhi was an Indian and a Hindu. Born in India, he spent some time in South Africa, where he was outraged at the inequalities of the system there.

During the 1930s and 1940s the British Army governed India. Gandhi returned home to an occupied country. He believed that the Indians must be free to govern themselves – but he maintained that it would be both wrong and impractical to use force against the British. Instead, Gandhi developed a very effective policy of non-cooperation and non-violent protest. He organised huge unarmed protest marches, and himself went on hunger strike.

In 1947 the British were forced out of India and it became an independent state. Only a year later, Gandhi was assassinated.

A   *Mahatma Gandhi*

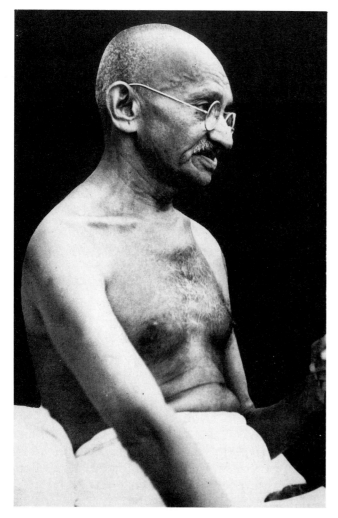

Martin Luther King (1929–1968)

B   *Martin Luther King*

Martin Luther King was a black American. He grew up in an America where blacks were treated as second-class citizens. Many had to live in poor conditions and were exploited by their white employers. They were treated unfairly on public transport, in shops and at work.

In the 1950s and '60s black people began to rise up in protest against the way they were treated. There were riots in several cities with large black populations.

By this time, Martin Luther King was working as a Christian minister. He was against the use of violence in campaigning for equality. He taught his followers to use the non-violent approach of Gandhi. He:

- organised boycotts of buses and shops where blacks were discriminated against;
- led black people throughout America on marches to protest against discrimination.

Largely as a result of these protests, many of the things Martin Luther King dreamed of came true – black children were allowed into schools with whites, black people could ride anywhere on a bus, all black people were allowed to vote in local elections ... But for Martin Luther King the dream had a tragic ending – like Gandhi, he was killed by an assassin.

---

1 Find out all you can about either Mahatma Gandhi or Martin Luther King. Write a brief biographical account including what you have found out.

Why is non-violent protest effective?

Any form of protest is designed to draw people's attention to a particular problem or issue. But violent protest is likely to upset, or alienate, many people. Non-violent action is more likely to win widespread public support. It challenges people to think about issues that they may not have considered before. This, in turn, puts pressure on those in authority and may force them to make changes, over time. In non-violent protest:

- laws may be broken – but this often serves to show how unfair or stupid the laws are;
- ordinary people can become involved – it is not just for extremists;
- people stand up for themselves and for what they believe in – they feel they have a part to play in changing society;
- the opposition is less effective – it is difficult to treat a person violently if they refuse to fight back.

---

2 If you wanted to protest about an issue, how would you go about it? Would you take violent action or use a non-violent approach? Why?

3 Can non-violent protest ever succeed in over-throwing injustice, or does violence always win in the end?

What does the Bible say?

Matthew 5.39
Do not resist one who is evil. But if any one strikes you on the right cheek, turn and offer him the other also.

Matthew 5.44
Love your enemies and pray for those who persecute you.

- Was Jesus recommending passive resistance here?

A matter of opinion

Archbishop Camara has led Christians in Brazil in non-violent protests for many years. He says:

I hereby make the donation of my person, physical and spiritual, to non-violent action.

To take non-violent action is to believe more firmly in truth, justice and love than in the power of falsehood, injustice and hatred.

- Do you think these words are full of hope, or pathetically idealistic?
- Why do you think that, as a Christian, Archibishop Camara is so firmly committed to non-violent action?

6.4 The death penalty

I think the death penalty should be restored – certainly for murder. We're too soft on criminals in this country. The death penalty would act as a deterrent. And it's only justice that a person who kills someone else should lose his own life.

Paul, 19

Do you agree with Paul? Surveys suggest that over 75% of the British population do. The majority of people would like to see the death penalty brought back – especially for terrorist crimes and the murder of policemen and young children.

Changes in the law

At the end of the 18th century in Britain a person could be sentenced to death for any one of over

200 offences. These 'capital' offences included stealing a loaf of bread or a sheep.

During the nineteenth and early twentieth centuries there were a number of reforms, and punishments became less severe. In 1957 the Government declared that only certain forms of murder should be punished by execution: killing during an armed robbery, killing policemen, using guns or explosives, and killing more than one person.

In 1965 Parliament suspended the death penalty for a trial period of five years, and it was abolished in 1970.

Arguments for and against capital punishment

For
1 Capital punishment is a tried and tested way of dealing with murderers – based on the old principle of justice: 'an eye for an eye, a tooth for a tooth'.
2 Unfortunately, some people in society can only understand the language of violence. Capital punishment is the only sort of deterrent they will understand.
3 Society has a duty to protect those who fight against crime – policemen, prison warders etc.
4 A so-called 'life' sentence may only last about 10 years – then the prisoner is released, perhaps to kill again.
5 The death penalty means that justice is *seen* to be done – family and friends of the murdered victim have a right to expect retribution.

Against
1 Only God has the right to give and take life.
2 How can we ever be absolutely sure that a person is guilty? It is likely that on more than one occasion in this century an innocent person has been hanged.
3 There is no reason to assume that the death penalty is a real deterrent to someone who is intent on murder.
4 To kill terrorists would turn them into martyrs and provoke even more extreme action.
5 The death penalty is barbaric. Most enlightened countries have abolished it. Those countries which still have the death penalty are often condemned for inhumane treatment.
6 The death penalty may be used indiscriminately, to dispose of a government's opponents. According to the Human Rights organisation, Amnesty International, 100 countries in the world still have the death penalty. Estimates of the number of people killed in the last decade range from 10,000 to 40,000.

---

1 Weigh up the arguments for and against the death penalty. Which do you think are the most convincing? Can you add any of your own arguments to either side?

Amnesty International has declared that the death penalty is a violation of the Declaration of Human Rights (see Unit 9.3). In the Declaration of Stockholm, issued following a conference on the abolition of the death penalty, in December 1977, Amnesty stated that the death penalty was:

A *the ultimate cruel, inhuman and degrading punishment and violates the right to life.*

It went on:

– *The death penalty is frequently used as an instrument of repression against opposition, racial, ethnic, religious and underprivileged groups,*
– *Execution is an act of violence and violence tends to provoke violence,*
– *The imposition and infliction of the death penalty is brutalizing to all who are involved in the process,*
– *The death penalty has never been shown to have a special deterrent effect,*
– *The death penalty is increasingly taking the form of unexplained disappearances, extra-judicial executions and political murders,*
– *Execution is irrevocable and can be inflicted on the innocent.*

---

2 Would you support Amnesty's campaign to ban the death penalty throughout the world? Say why/why not.
3 Does the State have the 'right' to take someone's life?

A matter of opinion

If I kill someone else, I forfeit my own right to live. The State is then quite justified in putting me to death.

Far from stamping out violence, the death penalty actually perpetuates the idea of violence and revenge, because it makes life seem cheap.

● Which of these statements do you agree with, and why?

ADDICTIONS
7.1 What is a drug?

The withdrawal symptoms are various and bizarre. They change from day to day ... It is rather like being hopelessly drunk. Normal life seems distanced and unreal. Mental processes are fogged and slow. At its worst it becomes impossible to construct a coherent sentence.

Mary, 32

The words of a hardened drug addict? No – Mary is a wife and mother trying to give up the tranquillisers she has taken for the last six years.

When was the last time you took an aspirin? You probably didn't think of it as 'taking drugs'. All of us take drugs from time to time. For some people, regular medication can literally mean the difference between life or death.

Drugs, then, have the power to heal – but they can also damage and destroy.

Where do drugs come from?

Some drugs come from plants. Opium, for example, comes from the opium poppy which grows in many Asian countries. Medicinal herbs and plants have been used by country people for centuries.

Today drugs can also be produced in the laboratory, by blending different chemicals. The drugs industry is a very profitable business. New 'wonder drugs' are constantly being developed.

Before a company can launch a product on to the market, it has to be rigorously tested. Scientists must look out for any potential side-effects, which may be harmful. Many of these tests are performed on animals, and some of them involve considerable suffering.

Sometimes, however, things can go disastrously wrong. In the 1960s, the drug Thalidomide was used to help pregnant women sleep. Doctors did not realise that Thalidomide had any side-effects – but it did terrible damage to the women's unborn babies.

---

1 Do you think it is fair to try out drugs on animals?

Everyday drugs

Tea as a drug? It may be surprising, but both coffee and tea contain caffeine, a stimulant, which can be addictive. Alcohol and coffee, too, are addictive, and if taken in large quantities they can damage or kill (see Unit 7.5).

---

2 'If tobacco and alcohol were discovered for the first time today, they would be banned at once.' Do you agree with this? Do you think more should be done to prohibit tobacco and alcohol abuse?

Drug dependence

A person who is seriously dependent on a drug becomes unable to cope without it. Dependence may be physical and/or psychological. And it is not only illegal or hard drugs which cause dependence or addiction (you can read more about these in Unit 7.2). Some people, like Mary, become addicted to tranquillisers or anti-depressant drugs first prescribed by a doctor. If you know someone struggling to give up smoking you will see how powerful an addiction to tobacco can be.

A person who is *physically* dependent on a drug will experience physical cravings for that substance. If they are deprived of the drug, they will suffer withdrawal symptoms, which only stop when they take more of the drug. As a person's body gets used to the drug, they may need to take more and more to avoid getting these unpleasant symptoms.

A person who is *psychologically* dependent begins to feel that they cannot cope without the drug. For example, someone who is prescribed sleeping

69

tablets may initially be relieved at getting a good night's sleep. If they are worried that they might not be able to sleep, it seems only natural to take a sleeping pill. And before long that person may be convinced that they can only sleep if they have taken one or more tablets.

Drug 'abuse' occurs whenever a person takes a drug for a non-medical reason (usually when it has not been prescribed by a doctor or bought at a chemists).

A matter of opinion

A British Government spokesman commented:

Drug abuse is a disease from which no country and no section of modern society seems immune. Stamping it out will be slow and painful ... The rewards if we succeed are great and the price of ultimate failure unthinkable.

---

3 How would you go about tackling the 'drug problem'?

A Drugs – the facts

- About 100,000 people die prematurely each year as a result of smoking.
- 700,000 people are thought to have a serious alcohol problem.
- Many drug addicts die from an accidental overdose or by infections (such as hepatitis) contracted by using unsterile needles.
- The number of people dying from heroin addiction and solvent abuse goes up each year.
- Around 500,000 people in this country have taken tranquillisers for seven years or more and can be considered dependent on them.

7.2 Drugs – the facts

You are at a party. One of your friends comes over and hands you a couple of tablets. 'Try this,' he says 'it's amazing ...' How do you react? What goes through your mind? Do you say yes – or no?

It may seem like quite an unimportant incident – but the decision you make could affect the rest of your life.

This is the way many young people first encounter illegal drugs. For a few, it is the first step to addiction, physical and mental deterioration, and possibly death.

Why do people take illegal drugs?

A whole range of complex factors may lead a person to become involved with drugs. They include:

- boredom – 'I did it for kicks'
- peer pressure – 'Everyone else does it ...'
- anxiety and tension – 'It helps me relax and forget my problems'
- personal problems – 'It makes me feel better about myself'
- novelty – 'I'll try anything once'

---

1 Can you think of any other factors to add to the list?

Illegal drugs – the risks

Few people, when they take drugs for the first time, are fully aware of the risks they run. **A** shows the most common illegal drugs used in Britain, and their effects. 'New' drugs, such as Crack or Ecstasy,

70

Amphetamines	Stimulate the body and its reactions. When this wears off, the user becomes very depressed. Taken in large quantities, over a long period, amphetamines can cause heart problems, malnutrition and death.
Cocaine	Has a similar effect to amphetamines. Is more likely to lead to dependence.
Heroin	Produces lethargy, apathy, loss of judgement and self-control. Since heroin is usually injected, users risk contracting hepatitis or AIDS from dirty needles.
Cannabis	Taken long-term can lead to confusion and hallucinations. Can also damage lung tissue.
LSD	Leads to hallucinations and feelings of panic. These may continue even after a person stops using the drug.
Solvents	Short-term use leads to hallucinations, confusion and accidental injury. Long-term use may cause damage to lungs, brain and liver.

A *Illegal drugs and their effects*

are usually made out of one or more of these. Crack, for example, is unrefined heroin. The risk is even higher with these drugs, since unscrupulous dealers may 'adulterate' the drug with other substances.

---

2 Do you think young people know enough about the dangers of drug abuse? How would you go about getting the message across?

How do drugs work?

When a drug is taken into the body – inhaled, swallowed, sniffed or injected – it rapidly passes into the bloodstream. The drug is carried to the brain and acts on the central nervous system. Different parts of the brain control different functions – a drug may affect someone's mood, behaviour, speech, sight or physical condition.

A person who becomes dependent on drugs may soon find it difficult to concentrate on their work. Before long, they may lose their job. Drugs are expensive, too. Many drug addicts turn to crime to finance their habit.

Helen's story

Extract **B** is taken from *Drugs. What every parent should know*, a booklet issued by the Institute for the Study of Drug Dependence.

B When 16 year old Helen broke off with her current boyfriend nobody thought much of it. It seemed a natural part of teenage life. But Helen was depressed and upset. She knew that when her mother felt that way she took Valium – a drug legally prescribed by the family doctor. So Helen tried it too, and it made her feel better. It wasn't long before her mother noticed that the Valium was disappearing and when she found a capsule in Helen's bedroom, she put two and two together.

Angry and frightened, she immediately told Helen's father. They confronted Helen together and a fierce argument followed. This ended with Helen slamming tearfully out of the house and the Valium being put under lock and key. This might have made sense earlier, but it was now too late to solve anything. The following week a schoolfriend gave Helen what was probably heroin, although neither of them were quite sure. Nevertheless, it seemed exciting and sophisticated and – better still – it was a way of getting back at her parents.

Later still, she took up with a new boyfriend, older than herself and a regular drug user. Helen's parents were unaware of their daughter's deeper involvement in the drug scene until they heard about the new boyfriend being arrested for a drug offence. Realising they were out of their depth, they decided to seek help from a family guidance counsellor.

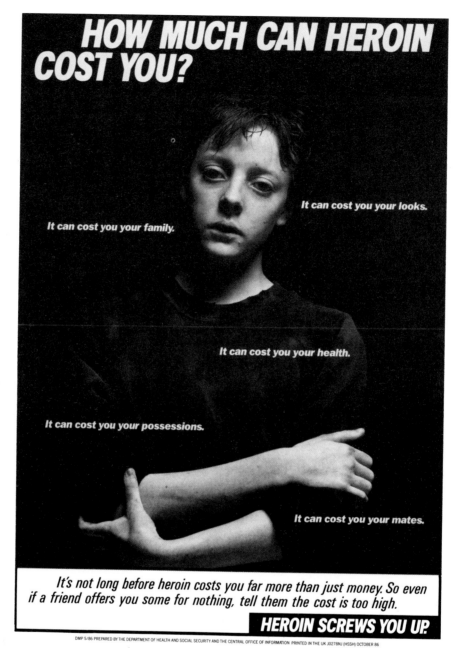

HOW MUCH CAN HEROIN COST YOU?

It can cost you your family.

It can cost you your looks.

It can cost you your health.

It can cost you your possessions.

It can cost you your mates.

It's not long before heroin costs you far more than just money. So even if a friend offers you some for nothing, tell them the cost is too high.

HEROIN SCREWS YOU UP

DMP 5/86 PREPARED BY THE DEPARTMENT OF HEALTH AND SOCIAL SECURITY AND THE CENTRAL OFFICE OF INFORMATION. PRINTED IN THE UK J0278NJ (HSSH) OCTOBER 86

C   *Do you think this is an effective warning against drug abuse?*

---

5 a) How did Helen get involved in drugs?
  b) Do you think her parents were wrong to react as they did? What else could they have done?
  c) What do you think will happen to Helen now?

A matter of opinion

When some young people were asked if they would take drugs, this is what they said:

Yes – why not? I don't see what all the fuss is about. Cigarettes and alcohol are just as bad.

No, I wouldn't touch drugs – I like to be in control of what I'm doing.

Just cannabis or something – none of the hard drugs …

Well, if everyone else was, I think I would find it hard to say no.

- Choose one of these points of view and write an imaginary conversation with the speaker.
- Design a poster like **C** warning young people of the dangers of drugs.

7.3 Drugs – coming off

For ages I refused to admit I had a drug habit. I thought I could come off whenever I liked ... But the heroin seemed to take control. Getting the next fix was the most important thing in my life.

Then the house where I was staying was raided by the police. I ended up in a treatment centre. Coming off was hell – physical and mental torture – but the staff were really good. I've been clean now for six months, and I'm determined never to touch drugs again.

Sean, 18

Withdrawal

If you have ever tried to go on a diet you'll know what it feels like to crave something. Withdrawal from addictive drugs is much, much worse. Depending on the seriousness of the addiction, the symptoms may range from severe nausea and acute depression to unconsciousness and coma.

There are now about 100 hospitals in the United Kingdom which have facilities to treat drug addicts. Some of these provide in-patient care, others run Drug Dependency Clinics. A person may attend voluntarily – following referral from their GP – or be compelled to attend by a court order, if they have been arrested for drug-related offences.

When an addict attends a clinic for the first time, he or she is given a thorough medical examination, and blood and urine samples are taken for analysis. When the addict's needs have been assessed, treatment can get underway.

There are two main methods of withdrawal:

1. Instant withdrawal, or 'cold turkey'. The addict simply stops taking the drug. This method can be effective, but the person may suffer very severe withdrawal symptoms.
2. Gradual 'weaning off'. Supplies of the drug may be cut down gradually, or the addict may be prescribed a substitute drug, which has less damaging effects. Heroin addicts, for example, may be given the drug methadone.

In many drug units and clinics addicts will also receive counselling and therapy to help them face life without drugs.

A matter for Christian concern

Many individual Christians and Christian organisations are involved in the fight against drugs and in the care and rehabilitation of drug addicts. Two Christian centres are:

Yeldall Manor, Reading, was set up in 1977 to treat male addicts between the ages of 18 and 35. The centre aims to help addicts by providing care in an atmosphere of love and discipline. Underlying this is a belief that commitment to God and Christ can help overcome the addiction.

Coke Hall Trust, in Hampshire, accepts men and women between the ages of 20 and 35 and offers them help and support to keep off drugs. People are expected to be drug-free on admission.

---

1 Do you think Christianity has anything to offer drug addicts? Why do you think Christians are involved in the fight against drugs?

A matter of opinion

The British Medical Association issued this comment by Gregory (19) a past heroin addict.

We used to take heroin together. When we decided to come off we had to support and encourage one another. We knew that if one of us continued, it wouldn't take long for the rest of us to start using again. We even started a self-help group near our estate with some of the other kids who wanted to come off. You've got to find things to do when you come off, something to keep you busy so you don't want that buzz again. I started thinking about what I really wanted to do. I started doing carpentry again, making a unit for my stereo, writing poetry about the things around me.

● Read what Gregory has to say again. Make notes on what you think are the key points in his campaign to give up drugs. Do you think he will succeed?

ADDICTIONS
7.4 Alcohol

Alcohol problem? Not me! I just like a drink, that's all ...

I can handle it – I know when I've had enough.

Just another half won't make any difference.

I like a glass of wine with a meal, maybe a sherry when I get home in the evening. There's no harm in that.

I got so drunk last week, I swore I'd never touch it again ...

I've been going into pubs since I was about 13.

I don't really like drinking, but all my friends drink...

My wife doesn't know I drink so much... I have to smuggle the bottles out of the house...

Which of these people would you say had a drinking problem? The answer could be all of them – or none of them.

Alcohol is part of everyday life. There are pubs and off-licenses on every high street; supermarkets sell alcohol; advertisements for alcohol appear on TV, in magazines and newspapers every day. National consumption of alcohol is now almost three times what it was in the 1950s. People in the United Kingdom spend £50,000,000 a day on alcoholic drinks.

---

1 Why do you think national consumption of alcohol has increased so rapidly?

An old habit

No-one knows when people first discovered how to produce alcohol. It was certainly well known to the ancient Greeks and Romans, who had a god of wine called Bacchus. The *Epic of Creation*, written in Babylonia in about 2225 BC had this to say about alcohol:

A *Sweet drink put far away their cares. As they drank liquor their bodies became satiated. Much they bubbled and their mood was exalted.*

Alcohol – the effects

Medical evidence seems to suggest that drinking alcohol in moderation is not harmful. In fact, some doctors go even further and say that an occasional drink can be good for us, since it helps us relax.

But how do we know when we have had enough? The answer is – we don't. Within half a minute of having a drink, some of the alcohol reaches the brain. There, it affects judgement and self-control – and maybe leads us to have 'just one more drink'. **B** looks at the effects of drinking alcohol.

74

The brain	Alcohol slows the brain down. Reaction time, judgement and self-control are affected (this is why it is so dangerous to drink and drive). Alcohol is a depressant. It may appear to make people more lively, but this is because it weakens their self-control.
	Too much alcohol can affect mood, speech, sight and balance – until a person becomes unconscious.
The liver	Alcohol is actually a poison. The liver is able to cope with small amounts of alcohol. But too much alcohol consumed over a long period may permanently damage the liver. It may even fail altogether – which can be fatal. The most common cause of death among alcoholics is cirrhosis of the liver.
The heart	Alcohol can damage and weaken the heart muscle, increasing the risk of heart failure. A heavy drinker may develop fatty deposits around the heart.
	Even a small amount of alcohol leads to higher blood pressure and a faster pulse rate, putting strain on the heart.
The stomach	Small amounts of alcohol can help the body digest food. Larger quantities may lead to cancer, stomach ulcers and muscle wastage.
The muscles	Steady drinking may destroy the co-ordination between the brain and different organs in the body.

B *The effects of alcohol abuse*

2 If alcohol is so bad for us, why do you think so many people drink?

Alcoholism

According to the World Health Organisation, around 7% of the world's population (1 in 16) is now dependent on alcohol. Many people refuse to admit they have an alcohol problem – even to themselves. The families of alcoholics also suffer. Organisations such as Alcoholics Anonymous exist to help alcoholics and their families overcome the problem.

The Christian view

Christians are divided over the use of alcohol. Some are firmly against it – they point to the dangers of alcohol abuse, and to the damage alcohol can do to relationships. In Victorian times, many young people 'signed the pledge' – promising that they would never touch alcoholic drink. Until very recently, members of the Methodist Church were not allowed to drink.

Other Christians argue that there is nothing wrong with drinking in moderation. They point out that Christ himself turned water into wine at the wedding celebration in Canaa.

3 Which viewpoint do you agree with, and why?

What does the Bible say?

Proverbs 23. 29–23
Do not look at wine when it is red,
when it sparkles in the cup
and goes down smoothly.
At the last it bites like a serpent,
and stings like an adder.
Your eyes will see stranger things,
and your mind utter perverse things.

● Is this a convincing warning about the dangers of alcohol abuse?

A matter of opinion

A Japanese proverb states:

First the man takes a drink, then the drink takes a drink, then the drink takes the man.

● Make up your own 'proverb' about alcohol abuse.

ADDICTIONS
7.5 Smoking

How would you explain smoking to a visitor from another planet? Something like this:

1 Roll a piece of paper into a tube.
2 Fill it with dried, shredded leaves.
3 Set light to it.
4 Place it between your lips.
5 Breathe in . . .

Put like this, the whole thing sounds rather strange, doesn't it? Yet one in four human beings does this several times every day!

Why do people smoke?

It calms me down, helps me relax . . .

I started because I wanted to look 'grown up' – now I can't stop.

All my friends smoke – they'd laugh if I said no.

It gives me something to do when I'm nervous . . .

My parents always smoked like chimneys. It just seemed like the natural thing to do . . .

Evidence suggests that most smokers begin before they are 16, even though it is illegal, in Britain, to sell cigarettes or tobacco to people under 16. Tobacco is addictive (see Unit 7.1) – once a person has become a regular smoker, it is very difficult to break the habit.

---

1 Ask five people you know who smoke:
  a How old they were when they first smoked.
  b Why they started.
  c If they have ever tried to give up.
  List their answers. Can you find any common pattern?
2 Why do you think so many people start smoking before they are 16? What arguments would you use to persuade young people not to smoke?

Smoking and health

When a person inhales (breathes in) tobacco smoke, a mixture of nicotine and carbon monoxide enters the blood-stream. The carbon monoxide stops the body getting its normal supply of oxygen; nicotine speeds up the heart-rate. Over time, deposits of tar collect in the air passages, in the lungs and on the teeth.

Each year over 50,000 people in Britain die from diseases related to smoking. That is eight times the number killed in fatal motor accidents. Most common causes of death among smokers are:

1 *Coronary heart disease* Each year 40,000 people under the age of 65 die from heart disease. About 75% of these deaths are linked with smoking.
2 *Cancer* 50 people a day die from lung cancer – 90% of these are smokers. All the evidence suggests that the nicotine and tar in cigarettes is 'carcinogenic' – that is, it creates the conditions that lead to cancer.
3 *Bronchitis and emphysema* You've probably heard someone with a smoker's cough. Many smokers develop chronic chest conditions which may eventually be fatal.

---

3 What more could be done to educate people about the dangers of smoking?

Risks to the non-smoker

Anyone who lives or works with a heavy smoker inevitably inhales some of the smoke, and may suffer some of the ill-effects involved. Some doctors suggest that as many as 1000 non-smokers are killed by smoke in Britain each year.

Recently, there have been increased campaigns to ban smoking in public places, such as buses, the Underground, offices and shops.

A *Would this poster put you off smoking?*

4 Do you think smoking should be banned in more places? Or is this a form of discrimination against smokers?
5 Are smokers selfish people?

in smoke' every day or week;
- thinking about the health risks;
- appreciating the benefits – better sense of taste and smell.

Giving up

Smoking is an addiction. Many people try very hard to give up – and fail repeatedly. Heavy smokers – like other 'drug' addicts – may experience unpleasant withdrawal symptoms. They may suffer more from stress, put on weight, become tired and irritable. A person who tries to give up smoking must, first of all, really want to succeed. Helpful strategies may be:

- using a substitute – such as herbal cigarettes or chewing gum;
- finding alternative ways of relaxing;
- avoiding places and situations where other people smoke;
- calculating the amount of money that 'goes up

A matter of opinion

... smoking is by far the largest avoidable hazard in Britain today and causes directly or indirectly up to 100,000 deaths a year ...

The cigarette is the most lethal instrument devised by man for peaceful use ...

They haven't really proved that smoking causes cancer. My grandfather lived to 90, and he'd been smoking since he was 12.

These days, everything seems to be bad for you ... We're always being told about pollution, contaminated food. It's just not worth worrying – there's nothing you can do about it.

- Which of these viewpoints do you find most convincing, and why?

ADDICTIONS
7.6 Gambling

A *Gambling – or just a harmless pastime?*

Gambling is an addiction – just like alcohol or drugs. I started playing the fruit machines when I was at school. Then when I got a job I used to spend all my pay at the betting shop. It's the excitement that hooks you. You're sure that this time you'll be lucky.

Kevin, 21

Have you ever bought a raffle ticket or taken part in a prize draw? If so, you have been gambling. That may surprise you. It seems a far cry from the glamorous world of casinos and night clubs we see on TV and films, or from the High Street betting shop.

Most people place some sort of bet occasionally. Passing five minutes at the local amusement arcade, or putting 50p on a Grand National runner seem like very harmless activities. But for a few people, what begins as a casual pastime can rapidly become an obsession.

The organisation Gamblers Anonymous was set up to help gamblers and their families. It estimates that there are now about 100,000 gambling 'addicts' in this country.

---

1 Do you find it surprising to hear gambling described as an illness or an addiction?

Why do people gamble?

Kevin pointed out that one of the attractions of gambling is excitement, the feeling that 'next time' you could be a winner. Gambling:

- lures people into a dream world, where they have the illusion of being rich and successful. According to Gamblers Anonymous, many gamblers have an inner urge to be powerful. Gambling allows them to escape, for a while, from their personal problems. Each time they lose, their problems become even more pressing, and so they are tempted to bet more and more.

78

- compulsive gamblers are often people who suffer from emotional insecurity. They may believe that winning a bet, or becoming rich, would transform their whole lives. Gambling offers a way of feeling in control of what happens to them. Each time someone like this places a bet, they feel that they will 'get lucky'.
- for many people, gambling is an antidote to boredom and loneliness. For young people like those in **A** the amusement arcades offer something to do – in the lunch hour, or when they should be at school.

---

2 Do you find gambling exciting? If so, try to explain why.

B Gambling – the facts

People in Britain are spending more and more on gambling. A recent survey found that:

- 39% of the adult population gambles regularly. Men are twice as likely as women to gamble.
- 35% of people fill in football pools regularly. 9% bet on horses or dogs at least once a month. 4% regularly play bingo.
- the 'typical' gambler is likely to be between 45 and 64, a manual worker, living in the north of England.
- teenage gambling is increasing. Two thirds of schools in the London area now face a serious gambling problem, mainly centred on fruit machines.

---

3 Do any of the findings in **B** surprise you? Which ones, and why?
4 Why do you think more men than women are involved in gambling?

Gambling – the consequences

Like any other addict, the compulsive gambler begins to need more and more of the 'drug' – or, in this case, the excitement and sense of power that gambling brings.

If the gambler loses, they immediately place another bet, convinced that this time they will be lucky. If they win, they use their winnings on still more bets, for higher stakes.

The addicted gambler will spend all their earnings on betting. Once these run out, they may use housekeeping money, family savings, or even steal to pay off their debts. Gambling may cause tensions and break ups in relationships, destroy business life and lead, in some cases, to suicide.

Christians and gambling

Some Christians are violently opposed to gambling and will refuse even to take part in a Church raffle. Others take a milder view, but are still very concerned about the unhappiness that gambling causes – both to the gambler and to the rest of the family.

What does the Bible say?

Paul's warning about the 'love of money' is appropriate here:

I Timothy 6.9,10
. . . those who desire to be rich fall into temptation, into a snare, into many senseless and hurtful desires that plunge men into ruin and destruction. For the love of money is the root of all evils; it is through this craving that some have wandered away from the faith . . .

- Do you think that Christians are right to condemn gambling, or is it, in most cases, a bit of harmless fun?

A matter of opinion

John is 17. He has just left school and works in a local factory.

My parents are strong church members. They brought me up to believe that gambling was always wrong. When I started work here, I was amazed at the gambling that went on. Some of the older men go to the betting shop every day. The younger lads usually go down to the amusement arcade at lunchtime, or play the fruit machines in our social club. Some of them spend all their pay on gambling.

Of course, people laugh at me when I won't join them. It's really difficult to explain why without sounding 'holier than thou'. And they are my friends, too. It's not as if they are wicked people! I don't know what to do. Perhaps if I just played the machines now and again they would stop picking on me.

- What do you think John should do? Should he give in, just once or twice? If so, what can he say to his parents? Or should he stick to his opinion that gambling is wrong? If so, what can he say to his friends? What would you do?

CONFLICT

8.I War

I don't understand it when people talk about 'peace-time'. What peace? Whenever you turn on the TV there are reports about bombings here, terrorist raids somewhere else ... I don't think there has ever been a time when people weren't fighting each other. It's part of human nature.

Khalid, 16

The human cost of war

Since the beginning of the twentieth century, about 100,000,000 people have died in war (**A**). Who are the casualties?

- In World War I (1914–1918) 95% of the casualties were soldiers.
- In World War II (1939–1945) over 50% of the dead were civilians.
- In the war in the Lebanon, which has been going on since 1982, about 90% of those killed have been civilians, many of them women and children.
- If a nuclear war broke out, whole towns and cities could be wiped out.

These horrifying figures do not include the millions of people seriously injured or maimed in war, nor those whose minds are affected.

The refugee problem

Civilians who become caught up in the conflict, or who live and farm in a war zone, are forced to leave their homes and possessions. The lucky ones may find shelter with friends or family in another country. Many, especially the very poor, face disease and starvation.

When the Russian army moved into Afghanistan in 1979, many people became homeless. By the time the occupying Russians left, in 1989, more than half the population had become refugees.

In Ethiopia, thousands died of disease and malnutrition in refugee camps during the early 1980s.

A *The human cost of war.*

Wars of many kinds

Since the last 'world' war ended in 1945, there have been over 150 wars throughout the world. **B** shows some of the main 'war zones' of the last 20 years. It is estimated that more than 20,000,000 people have died in these conflicts — most of them women and children.

It is possible to group these wars into categories:

1 *Frontier disputes* Sometimes, two countries lay claim to an area of land on the border between them. Each demands that the frontier is re-drawn, neither will give way, until fighting breaks out. Many such disputes are between developing countries, as a result of the old colonial era. In the 19th century, European powers literally 'divided up' areas between them. These former colonies have gradually become independent and refuse to accept such artificial boundaries.

80

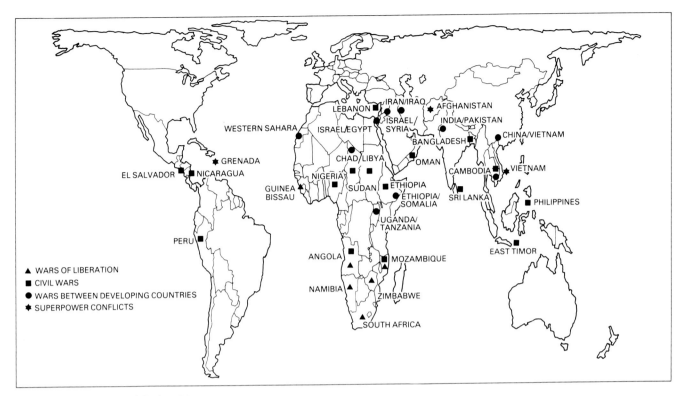

B *Major war zones of the last 20 years.*

Sometimes the dispute is over water, rather than land. For example, there has been a long-standing dispute between Greece and Turkey over part of the Aegean Sea. Both sides claim the area, which holds large deposits of oil and gas.

2 *Civil wars* and *wars of liberation* Different groups within a country may disagree to such an extent that they begin fighting – often for control of the country. For example at the beginning of 1989 there were civil wars in Sudan, Afghanistan, and El Salvador. Often the world's superpowers (USSR and USA) become involved in these internal disputes, providing the combatants with arms and finance. Some civil wars are 'unofficial'. Many people, for example, would describe the situation in Northern Ireland as civil war.

3 *Wars between nations* Wars between countries often arise because of frontier disputes, because of different political beliefs, or because one country lays claim to another. Since 1945, there have been wars in the Middle East and south East Asia. They include the Korean War (1950–53); the Vietnam War (1965–1973) and the Gulf War between Iran and Iraq (1980–1988). Millions have died as a result of these wars. As with civil wars, the superpowers were deeply involved in these conflicts.

---

1 Do you think that an outside power has the right to be involved in disputes within a country or between countries?

2 Does anyone 'win' a war?

A matter of opinion

If a person intends to kill you, be first to kill him.
(Jewish Talmud)

Fight in the way of Allah (GOD) with those who fight you but do not begin hostilities.
(Muslim Quran)

● According to these quotations, when is a person justified in going to war?

81

CONFLICT

8.2 Attitudes towards war

This unit contains a number of different accounts of war: an extract from the Old Testament Psalms, a diary entry, a poem, a newspaper article, a photograph and a piece from the New Testament.

Look at each item carefully. Think about:

1 The person who wrote (or photographed) it:
   • What had they experienced?
   • What were their feelings?
   • What view of war were they putting across?
   • What was their purpose in writing?

2 Your own reactions:
   • Did you find the item exciting? frightening? depressing?
   • Did it influence the way you felt about war?

Using one of the items as a starting-point, write your own description of war, and how you feel about it.

Psalm 18, 31–41

For who is God, but the Lord?
And who is a rock, except our God? – the God who girded me with strength, and made my way safe.
He made my feet like hinds' feet, and set me secure on the heights.
He trains my hands for war, so that my arms can bend a bow of bronze.
Thou hast given me the shield of thy salvation, and thy right hand supported me, and thy help made me great.
Thou didst give a wide place for my steps under me, and my feet did not slip.
I pursued my enemies and overtook them; and did not turn back till they were consumed.
I thrust them through, so that they were not able to rise; they fell under my feet.
For thou didst gird me with strength for the battle; thou didst make my assailants sink under me.
Thou didst make my enemies turn their backs to me, and those who hated me I destroyed.
They cried for help, but there was none to save, they cried to the Lord, but he did not answer them.
I beat them fine as dust before the wind; I cast them out like the mire of the streets.

Little Johnny Jones,
He was a US pilot,
And no shrinking vi'let
Was he.
He was mightly proud
When World War Three
Was declared.
He wasn't scared.
No siree!
And this is what he said on
His way to Armageddon:
'So long, mom,
I'm off to drop the bomb,
So don't wait up for me.
But though I may roam.
I'll come back to my home,
Although it may be
A pile of debris.
Remember, mommy,
I'm off to get a commie,
So send me a salami,
And try to smile somehow.
I'll look for you
When the war is over,
An hour and a half from now.'

The great moment had come. The curtain of fire lifted from the front trenches. We stood up. We moved in step, irresistibly, towards the enemy lines. I was boiling with a mad rage which had taken hold of me and all the others in this incomprehensible fashion. The overwhelming wish to kill gave wings to my feet. The monstrous desire for annihilation which hovered over the battlefield thickened the brains of men in a red fog. We called each other in sobs, and stammered disconnected sentences. A neutral observer might have perhaps believed we were seized by an excess of happiness.

Ernst Junger, *Diary*. 1918

A paratroop lieutenant has described the reason why a large number of British officers joined the army. "Oh, too many comics, the idea of running around with a submachine gun and rather relishing the idea of being shot at . . . It's a pity to have gone through life without ever having done anything more dangerous than crossing the road.
Martin Woolacott. 'Changing the guard'. *The Guardian* 10.7.73

Matthew 5.38
You have heard that it was said, 'You shall love your neighbour and hate your enemy'. But I say to you, Love your enemies and pray for those who persecute you, so that you may be sons of your Father who is in heaven.

8.3 Nuclear weapons

It's all very well shouting 'Ban the bomb!'. But what would all these pacifists do if World War Three broke out? If we don't get the enemy first, they'll get us. In the end it will all depend on who has the biggest stock of nuclear arms.

Tony, 35

---

1 Do you agree with Tony's argument? If not, how would you answer him?

The Arms Race

In 1945, only America possessed the 'secret' of how to manufacture nuclear arms. They used this knowledge to produce the atomic bombs which were dropped on Hiroshima and Nagasaki, ending the Second World War.

It was not long, however, before other countries developed the knowledge and technology necessary to produce their own nuclear weapons. The essential ingredient is plutonium. This is produced by nuclear reactors. Any country with nuclear generators, used for power, has the capacity to manufacture its own nuclear weapons.

The so-called 'arms race' really began in 1949, when the USSR developed and tested its own nuclear weapons. After this, both sides raced to develop more powerful and sophisticated weapons, and to stock-pile supplies of arms.

There are now five main runners in the 'arms race': US, USSR, UK, France and China. Of these, the USSR and the US are still the front runners. However at least 12 other countries, including Israel and Pakistan, are thought to have the knowledge to make nuclear weapons. A further 20 countries could obtain the necessary knowledge and technology in the next 10 years.

Nuclear deterrence

Supporters of nuclear arms usually argue that they act as a 'deterrent': 'If the other side goes on piling up arms, we must too. That way we will maintain a balance and neither side will dare attack the other.'

The argument sounds logical. But how much is enough? America and Russia each have about 200 cities with a population over 200,000. It would take only two nuclear warheads to destroy each of these cities. So only 400 warheads could wipe out more than 100,000,000 people on each side.

Yet both America and Russia each possess more than 10,000 warheads. Is this deterrence, or 'over-kill'?

---

2 Do you agree that nuclear arms act as a deterrent?

3 Why do you think that America and Russia possess far more nuclear weapons than they seem to need?

How could a nuclear war start?

In the 45 years since the end of World War II the world has avoided a nuclear war. Supporters of nuclear arms feel that the 'balance' of nuclear weapons has helped maintain this peace. Since the major powers know how to manufacture arms, they say, it would be pointless trying to ignore them. The fact that the devastation caused by nuclear war would be so terrible has actually helped prevent such a conflict. Besides, there are strict safeguards to avoid any 'accidental' use of nuclear weapons.

Opponents of nuclear weapons feel that it is only a matter of time. With so many nuclear weapons 'lying around' it is inevitable that someone, one day, will want to use them. They point out that a modern nuclear bomb is more than a thousand times more powerful than the one dropped on Hiroshima, which killed a total of 64,000 people.

Why don't they give **us** useful jobs instead of **them** preparing for nuclear war?

A How many jobs does the bomb cost?
Explain in your own words what point this cartoon is making.

A full-scale nuclear war between the US and the USSR (which would involve allies of these countries, such as the UK) could start if:

- one country planned a deliberate first strike and took the other by surprise;
- a war fought with conventional weapons escalated into a major conflict;
- a technical error set off a missile accidentally;
- an irresponsible government or terrorist group got hold of nuclear weapons;
- a madman or dictator came to power in one of the major arms-holding countries and disregarded the safety precautions.

As well as the threat of destruction, the stock-piling of nuclear arms costs billions of pounds (**A**).

---

3 Do you think possession of large stocks of nuclear weapons makes a nuclear war more or less likely? Give reasons for your answer.
4 What point is cartoon **A** making? Do you agree?

A matter of opinion

Nuclear deterrence has kept the peace for 40 years and a non-nuclear world would be much more dangerous. The temptation for the superpowers to use some of the many nasty conventional chemical or biological weapons at their disposal would be increased, which would leave Western Europe very vulnerable indeed to Soviet attack.

Editorial in *The Sunday Times*, 19.1.1986

Before the bomb, man had to live with the idea of his death as an individual; from now onwards, mankind has to live with the idea of death as a species.

Arthur Koestler

The world now stands on the brink of the final abyss.

Lord Mountbatten

- Do you agree or disagree with each of these statements?

85

8.4 Disarmament

The only way to stop the arms race is for each country, individually, to say 'No' to nuclear weapons and get rid of its stockpile of arms. If we always wait for the other side to move first, we'll never have a safer world.

Nita, 19

Nita is a *unilateralist* (see below) and a member of CND. Many people would see her approach as hopelessly idealistic, if not stupid. Yet what other options are available?

1   *The retentionists* This group believes that the USSR is not to be trusted. The West should hold or retain as many weapons as the 'enemy' in order to keep the balance of power.

---

1 Look back at what you read about the arms race in Unit 8.3. How would the retentionists' view affect the race?

---

2   *The multilateralists* Multilateralists believe that both sides should negotiate over arms. Some feel that the answer lies in a single treaty, in which all countries would agree to reduce their stockpile of arms. Others favour the gradual reduction of weapons, through a series of agreements. So far, nuclear weapons have been banned in Antarctica and Latin America, in outer space and on the sea bed. In 1987 the US and USSR agreed to destroy medium and short-range nuclear missiles within three years, and to allow each other open inspection of nuclear weapon sites.

---

2 Do you think that either of these approaches could work? Would newly-arming countries agree to give up their stocks of arms?

---

3   *The bilateralists* This group suggests that the main effort towards disarmament must come from the US and USSR, since these possess 95% of all nuclear weapons. The US and USSR should come to an agreement that they will not develop, test or manufacture any more weapons – (a nuclear 'freeze'). The two sides could then negotiate the destruction of the weapons they do possess.

A *A CND poster protesting against the presence of American nuclear weapons in Britain.*

Just when you thought the world was getting safer ... Just when the superpowers are starting to disarm ...

along comes

TRIDENT

3 Do you think the US and USSR would agree to this sort of action?

4 *The unilateralists* Members of CND, like Nita, and other unilateralist groups argue that every country which has nuclear weapons, including Britain, should disarm – no matter what anyone else does.

4 Do you think the unilateralists are right? Or is this a stupidly idealistic view?

The great disarmament debate

Negotiate or take unilateral action? Opponents of nuclear arms, as we have seen, have very different views on how disarmament could be achieved.

Multilateralists
- Peace and freedom must be defended.
- Even if countries like the UK destroyed their nuclear weapons, there would be no guarantee that others would.
- If Britain destroyed its nuclear weapons it would have to rely on the US for protection.
- The nuclear deterrent has kept the peace for many years.
- What matters most is how governments behave.
- If a country has no nuclear weapons, it is an open invitation to others to attack.

Unilateralists
- Nuclear weapons cause such terrible destruction. It might be better to accept defeat, rather than use them.
- The huge stocks of nuclear weapons in the world are a threat to the entire human race. There is only one solution: to destroy them as soon as possible.
- Countries which have disarmed have not been invaded.
- Britain should give a moral lead to the world.

5 Can you add any arguments to either side of the disarmament debate? Which side do you agree with?

B *Christian CND protesters. Do you think Christians are right to become involved in controversial issues, or should religion and politics be kept apart?*

A matter of opinion

Many Christians are opposed to nuclear arms (**B**). Others feel they are a necessary evil.
Nuclear weapons are totally evil. How can Christians support the bomb when they see the terrible destruction it causes? Surely there's enough suffering in the world?

It's no use denying that nuclear weapons exist. As Christians, we must campaign for them to be used responsibly. But we owe it to our children – and to their children – to ensure that the country is well defended.

- Which do you think is the most 'Christian' viewpoint, and why?

CONFLICT

8.5 A just war?

Can war or violent struggle ever be just?
War or violent struggle can never be just except in the very special circumstances that it is the only way of restraining a very great injustice; that it will not itself bring about greater destruction than the evil it opposes; that it has a reasonable chance of success; that it does not involve acts of injustice such as the deliberate killing of non-combatants and that those who wage it are authorised to do so by a large degree of popular support.

Hebert, *The Teaching of the Catholic Church*

---

1 Do you think that any war could meet all the requirements in **A**? Is there such a thing as a 'just' war?

Most people feel that war and fighting should be avoided if at all possible. But few would call themselves 'pacifists' – that is, would refuse to fight at all, whatever the circumstances. The need to find some sort of middle way has led people to try to define what makes a *just* war.

This question has worried many Christians over the centuries. In AD 1250 Thomas Aquinas laid down four conditions which he felt justified a war and would enable a Christian to fight in God's name.

Condition 1 There must be a just cause for the war. In practice, this can only be when a country has been attacked.

Condition 2 Every other possibility must have been explored before war is declared – this means that the country's ruler must attempt to negotiate.

Condition 3 The war must have a just aim and all fighting must stop when that aim has been achieved.

Condition 4 The war must be fought in a just way: only as much force as is needed to bring about victory must be used; no violence must be directed towards civilians.

---

2 Can you think of any problems in meeting these conditions? Do you think that they could be applied to a modern conflict – for example, a nuclear war? Explain your answer.

A holy war

If an army or a country is convinced that it is fighting a 'just' war and that its cause is right, it may claim that it is fighting a 'holy war' and that it has 'God on its side'.

When the Roman Emperor Constantine became a Christian, he had a standard with a cross on it carried before his army. He was convinced that God enabled him to win against overwhelming odds.

Christian soldiers who took part in the Crusades in the Middle Ages believed that they were fighting for God against the 'infidels' or 'pagans' who had taken over the Holy Land.

It is not only Christians who argue that God is with them. Some Muslim extremists also believe that they should fight a 'holy war' against the West.

---

4 Do you think that any side in a war can claim that it is in the right? Explain your answer.

What does the Bible say?

Luke 14.31,32
... what king, going to encounter another king in war, will not sit down first and take counsel whether he is able with ten thousand to meet him who comes against him with twenty thousand? And if not, while the other is yet a great way off, he sends an embassy and asks terms of peace.

- What does this quotation tell us about the concept of a just war?
- Can you match up these extracts with Aquinas' four conditions?

HUMAN RIGHTS

9.1 The United Nations

A   We the peoples of the United Nations determine:

- to save succeeding generations from the scourge of war, and
- to reaffirm faith in fundamental human rights, in the dignity and worth of the human person, in the equal rights of men and women and of nations large and small, and
- to promote social progress and better standards of living.

And for these ends:

- to practise tolerance and to live together in peace with one another as good neighbours, and
- to unite our strength to maintain international peace and security, and
- to ensure, by the acceptance of principles and the institution of methods, that armed force shall not be used, save in the common interest, and
- to employ international machinery for the promotion of the economic and social advancement of all peoples.

Preamble to the Charter of
the United Nations

When the First World War ended in 1918, many of those involved were determined that such a tragic waste of life should never happen again. A group of nations combined to form the League of Nations in 1920. The League had no army of its own, but relied on persuasion and negotiation. The US never joined the League and the USSR withdrew in 1939. The League failed to stop the outbreak of the Second World War and was finally dissolved in April 1946.

By this time, however, a new peace-keeping organisation was being formed. It became known as the United Nations – a name thought up by the US President Roosevelt in 1942. Representatives of 51 countries (including the USSR) met in San Francisco in 1945. A is part of the Charter they drew up.

---

1 In your own words, list the objectives of the United Nations.

How does the UN work?

B explains the aims of the UN:

B   *To achieve international co-operation in solving international problems of an economic, social, cultural or humanitarian character, and in promoting and encouraging respect for human rights and for fundamental freedoms for all without distinction as to race, sex, language or religion . . .*

Delegates of the member states work together in a number of councils and agencies to achieve these aims. These include:

The General Assembly – the governing body of the UN. This meets at the UN headquarters in Geneva. All member countries can elect one representative to the General Assembly.

The Security Council – this body exists to keep the peace wherever it is threatened. Five countries: the US, USSR, UK, France and China – are permanent members of the Council. There are eight more places – the other countries take it in turns to belong.

The International Court of Justice which meets in the Hague, capital of the Netherlands. This Court settles legal disputes between countries. It also acts as a court of appeal.

The Food and Agricultural Organisation (FAO) This is mainly concerned with world food supplies and agricultural development in Third World countries. FAO projects include the fight against locusts in South America, improving irrigation and farming in South East Asia, and dealing with food emergencies and droughts.

The International Children's Emergency Fund (UNICEF) which concentrates on the needs of children throughout the world – especially victims of war, epidemics, hunger and disease. In recent years UNICEF has vaccinated 280,000,000 children against tuberculosis, and treated another 32,000,000 children for malaria.

The Relief and Works Agency (UNRWA) helps millions of refugees throughout the world

The World Health Organisation (WHO) works to combat disease and illness. 75% of the world's population cannot reach a doctor. Over 80% are out of reach of a dentist.

Other UN agencies include the International Atomic Energy Agency, the Disarmament Commission, the Emergency Force and Regional Economic Commissions.

---

2 Find out as much as you can about the different agencies of the UN and the work they do.
3 Which do you think is the most important of the UN's agencies? Why?

How successful is the UN?

It is almost impossible to measure the success of an organisation like the UN. Certainly there has not been a major world conflict since the Second World War. The UN sends peace-keeping forces to areas of conflict, such as the Middle East. UN agencies bring relief to millions of suffering people throughout the world. Different agencies and councils do at least encourage countries to talk to one another.

However, there are many critics of the UN. The US (which provides 30% of the organisation's income) is quick to point out its faults. Certainly during the 45 years since the UN was formed the world has become a much more dangerous place. We have only to pick up a newspaper or turn on the TV to hear of terrorist attacks, newer, more deadly weapons and political disagreements. Over 150 wars have been fought, there have been famines and disasters . . .

---

4 On balance, do you think the United Nations is a success or a failure?
5 Over the next few weeks, watch the news and look in newspapers and magazines for items on the UN. Make a folder about the UN's activities.
6 What world problems would you like to see the UN tackling in the next decade?

9.2 The Universal Declaration of Human Rights

On 10 December 1948 the United Nations drew up its Declaration of Human Rights. **A** shows just some of the statements in the Declaration. Member countries of the United Nations believe that every human being on earth is entitled to these civil, political, social and religious rights.

---

1 Read through **A**. Do any of the 'rights' surprise you? Which ones and why?
2 **a)** In pairs, choose what you think are the three most important rights in **A**. Work out and write down why you think these are the most important.
   b) Get together as a class and draw up a rank order of rights (use a flipchart or blackboard). For example, if 20 people thought that Article 18 was the most important, that might go at the top of your list, and so on.
   c) As a class, draw up an explanation of why you think this is the most important Human Right.

A The Declaration of Human Rights

Article 1 All human beings are born free and equal in dignity and rights.

Article 2 Everyone is entitled to these human rights without any distinction of race, colour, sex or religion.

Article 3 Everyone has the right to life, liberty and security of person.

Article 4 No-one shall be held in slavery.

Article 5 No-one shall be subjected to torture.

Article 7 All are equal before the law.

Article 11 Everyone charged with a criminal offence is presumed innocent until proved guilty.

Article 13 Everyone has the right to freedom of movement.

Article 16 Men and women of a full age have the right to marry and have a family.

Article 18 Everyone has the right to freedom of thought, conscience and religion.

Article 19 Everyone has the right to freedom of opinion and expression.

Article 20 Everyone has the right to peaceful assembly.

Article 23 Everyone has the right to work.

Article 24 Everyone has the right to rest and leisure.

Article 26 Everyone has the right to education.

Thousands are in prison because of their beliefs.

Help them. Help us.
Amnesty International

amidst a deafening silence from some of the very same people who pay lip service to the Universal Declaration of Human Rights.

... Amnesty's sole reason for existence (is) to campaign against torture and execution and for the release of men and women imprisoned for their beliefs, colour, ethnic origins, language or religion ... it is the inalienable right of people to exercise freedom of speech, association or organisation without fear ...

Fighting for human rights

Although many countries agree with the principles of the Declaration of Human Rights, they do not always act accordingly. Even countries which are members of the United Nations are sometimes accused of actions which go against the Declaration — for example, discriminating against minorities, censoring freedom of expression, or even torture.

The organisation Amnesty International fights for human rights throughout the world. **B** is how Amnesty describes its aims:

B *Amnesty International is engaged in what is very often a life or death struggle to defend human rights in many countries all over the world ... only by becoming a mass movement for human rights can we hope to play our full part in ending the international hypocrisy which surrounds the plight of so many — those who suffer alone or collectively*

3 Would this persuade you to join Amnesty International? Why/Why not?

4 Do you know of any cases in which people seem to have been denied their 'human rights'? Write notes on what happened.

A matter of opinion

The Universal Declaration of Human Rights adopted on 10 December 1948 promised a better world. The aspirations set out in its thirty articles, however, remain largely unfulfilled. The rights to life, to an adequate standard of living, to freedom of expression, to protection from torture, inhuman treatment, or arbitrary arrest, and many of the 'common standards of achievement for all peoples and nations' are as far from realisation as ever.

Prince Sadruddin Aga Khan.

● In the next week, look at newspapers and magazines and try to find three examples to support this view.

9.3 Human Rights: Valeri Barinov

As we saw in Unit 9.2, the Declaration of Human Rights is based on the principle that *every person in the world* is equal, and is entitled to the same things. Yet in many countries thousands of people are denied their 'human rights'. They may be imprisoned without trial, tortured, persecuted for their religious or political beliefs. In recent years Albania, Bulgaria, the Ivory Coast, Iraq, Iran, Indonesia and Turkey have been criticised for their human rights record.

This unit looks at one country and one man. The country is the USSR and the man is Valeri Barinov, a Christian rock musician.

According to Alexander Solzhenitsin, a Russian writer and human rights campaigner, 65 million Russians have been killed by their own leaders since 1923. Countless others have been exiled to labour camps or locked up in psychiatric hospitals like **A** because of their beliefs. One of them was Valeri Barinov.

Valeri Barinov

Valeri Barinov was arrested in 1984 and charged with trying to cross the Russian border illegally.

After a trial lasting three days, Barinov was found guilty. He was sentenced to 2 ½ years in a labour camp.

The Russian news agency, *Tass*, however, suggested that Barinov's real crime was that he had for several years:

B ... *maintained contact with foreigners – representatives of anti-Soviet organisations abroad. (With) the help of emissaries of those organisations, Barinov had tried to smuggle slanderous information abroad on the position of religious believers in the USSR.*

Tass Report 23.11.84

According to the news agency, therefore, Barinov was guilty of having 'openly conducted religious propaganda'.

Background

The Russian Communist leader Lenin (1870–1924) attacked all religious belief. He declared that:

C *All modern religions and churches ... serve to defend the exploitation of the people and stupefy*

A

the working class ... Every religious idea, every idea of God, is unutterable vileness.

This conflict between state and religion continues in the USSR. Between 50 and 80 million Soviet citizens (out of a population of around 270 million) are religious. This number includes Moslems, Jews, members of the Russian Orthodox Church, Baptists and Catholics.

The Soviet Constitution allows people to believe in religion, but not to teach or spread their beliefs. Religious people are viewed with suspicion and risk persecution or imprisonment. Anyone suspected of propaganda – for example, giving people religious books or Bibles, or encouraging them to join religious groups – may be arrested and severely punished.

Life in prison

At first, Barinov was held in Kresty prison in Leningrad. From there he was moved to psychiatric hospital, and then on to the KGB headquarters at Leitny Bridge.

During his imprisonment Barinov went on hunger strike as a protest. The first strike lasted 22 days. Barinov's health deteriorated rapidly, but once he had recovered he went on another hunger strike. He demanded to be allowed to leave Russia with his family. Barinov was force-fed, and it is believed that this brought on a heart attack.

Barinov appealed against his sentence, but the appeal was turned down. He was then sent to a labour camp. Camp 27, Barinov's new home, was nicknamed 'blood-soaked 27' because of the beatings and killings that took place there.

Release

By this time news of Barinov's plight had reached the outside world. A campaign was launched to pressurise the Russian authorities to release him. British politicians such as David Steel and Neil Kinnock signed an appeal and sent it to the Russian leader, Mr Gorbachev. The House of Commons passed a motion which stated (D):

D *No evidence was produced at his trial to support the charges and his trial concentrated on the activities of his Christian rock group.*

Barinov was released on 4 September 1986 and allowed to leave Russia (E).

E *Valeri Barinov with his wife Tanya, a few days after his release.*

1 Why do you think the Russian leaders are against religious belief?
2 Why might they view someone like Barinov as a threat? (Think about the influence rock musicians have in this country.)
3 Where do you think Barinov gained the strength to stand up for what he saw as his 'rights'?

What does the Bible say?

Let every person be subject to the governing authorities. For there is no authority except from God, and those that exist have been instituted by God. Therefore he who resists the authorities resists what God has appointed, and those who resist will incur judgement.

For rulers are not a terror to good conduct, but to bad. Would you have no fear of him who is in authority? Then do what is good, and you will receive his approval ...

Romans 13.1–3

● How do these words apply to the situation in Russia?
● Should a Russian Christian 'submit' to the authorities, or follow their conscience, like Barinov?
● How do you think a Russian Christian might reply to this?

9.4 The Rights of the Child

Spare the rod and spoil the child.

Children should be seen and not heard.

The usual age at which boys begin is from six upwards. They are generally the children of the poorest and worst-behaved parents who want to get rid of them and make a little money by it as well . . . Many of them get stuck and are taken out dead. They are smothered for want of air and the fright and at staying so long in the flue.

Children's Employment Commission, 1863

---

1 What view of childhood do these quotations give you? Do they suggest that children have any rights?

Until the early years of this century the idea of children having 'rights' would have seemed ridiculous to most people in Britain. Children were often viewed as their parents' property, unable to speak or think for themselves. Many children were forced to work long hours in mines and factories.

In 1922 Eglantyne Jebb, founder of Save the Children Fund, drafted a Charter of the Rights of the Child (**A**). In it, she spelled out what she believed were the rights of every child in the world, regardless of nationality, race or religion:

A

---

1 No child should be exploited.
2 Every child should be given the opportunity to mature physically, mentally and emotionally.
3 Each child should be taught to offer a life of service to others.

---

2 Re-write these statements in your own words.
3 What do you think Eglantyne Jebb meant by 'a life of service'. Do you agree?

In 1959 the United Nations (see Units 9.1 and 9.2) adopted its own Declaration of the Rights of the Child. It began by saying that 'mankind owes to the child the best it has to give'. Then the Declaration went on (**B**):

B Every child has the right to expect:

- special protection to allow them to grow physically, spiritually, socially and emotionally.
- a name and a nationality.
- adequate nutrition, education and medical services.
- special medical treatment if this is needed.
- love, care and protection, from parents or some other responsible body.
- protection in times of disaster and from all forms of cruelty and neglect.
- protection from any form of discrimination based on race or religion.

---

3 Do you agree that 'mankind owes to the child the best it has to give'? Why?
4 Rank the points of the Declaration in order of importance, from 1 to 7. Explain why you chose your three most important statements.
5 Is there anything you would add to the Declaration of the Rights of the Child?

Protection

Four of the UN's statement include the word 'protection'. Babies and very young children are helpless. They depend on adults and those around them, since they cannot speak or act for themselves. Until you leave school and can earn enough to support yourselves, it is likely that you, too, will have to depend on your parents or guardians.

In drafting its Declaration of the Rights of the Child the UN had three particular dangers in mind:

1 *War* Modern warfare does not distinguish between soldiers and civilians. Millions of women and children have been killed in recent wars. Those children who escape may be orphaned and homeless. War deprives them of a normal childhood and may leave them physically and mentally scarred.

2 *State terror* In many countries children are arrested, tortured and even killed. They may be held hostage or imprisoned because of their parents' religious or political beliefs. Amnesty International reported that at least 300 children were held hostage and tortured in Iraq in 1977. Many children are imprisoned in South Africa.

3 *Exploitation and abuse* 1979 was the International Year of the Child. Campaigners for Children's Rights revealed horrifying stories of children being exploited. Millions of children are forced to beg on the streets or become prostitutes to earn a living. Others work long, hard hours in sweatshops, as domestic servants or in forced labour camps. In the UK there are strict laws about employing children, but no such legislation applies in many parts of the world.

Child abuse may take many forms. Every year we read tragic stories of neglect or 'baby battering'. The sexual abuse of children and young people is also a serious problem. Some estimates put the number of children abused in this way as high as 1 in 10.

Who helps?

Many national and international organisations campaign to protect the rights of the child. Among the most famous are:

Amnesty International – As part of its fight for universal human rights, Amnesty takes a special interest in the rights of the child.

Save the Children Fund – This charity provides money and personnel to look after the long-term needs of children in many parts of the world. It also responds when children are involved in any emergency or disaster – such as the famine in Ethiopia in the 1980s.

The National Society for the Prevention of Cruelty to Children (NSPCC) – The NSPCC was founded in London in 1884. It works to protect and care for children in Britain: fundraising, mounting educational projects, setting up family care centres and child protection schemes. The NSPCC's Child Protection Officers may be called in to investigate cases

C *Photographs like this from the NSPCC illustrate the horrors of child abuse.*

of suspected child abuse (C). In 1987–88, the NSPCC helped 48,070 children.

6 Do you think that children need a special Declaration of Rights? Why?

What does the Bible say?

Matthew 18. 2,3
... calling to him a child, he put him in the midst of them, and said, 'Truly, I say to you, unless you turn and become like children, you will never enter the kingdom of heaven. Whoever humbles himself like this child, he is the greatest in the Kingdom of heaven.

"Whoever receives one such child in my name receives me; but whoever causes one of these little ones who believe in me to sin, it would be better for him to have a great millstone fastened round his neck and to be drowned in the depth of the sea.'

- What child-like qualities do you think Jesus had in mind when he told his disciples to 'become like children'?
- What does Jesus have to say about the need to protect children?

9.5 The Rights of Women

I don't consider myself to be a hard-line feminist, and I'm not anti-men. But I resent being treated like a second-class citizen. I work just as hard as the men in my office, so I've a right to equal pay and equal chances of promotion. Yet all the managers are men. When I complained, my boss said, 'Oh, you'll go off and start a family in a few years.' I was furious!

Carole, 27

If Carole can prove that she is not getting promotion because she is a woman, she could take her boss to court. Since the 1975 Sex Discimination Act, it has been illegal to discriminate against women in 'work, leisure and education'.

The background

The 1975 Act was the latest in a series of legislation designed to protect the rights of women. Until the end of the 19th century, British women had few legal rights. They were seen almost as pieces of 'property' – belonging first to their fathers and then to their husbands. Women could not vote or own property. It was very difficult for a woman to lead an independent life. Gradually, however, the situation began to change (**A**).

Women have welcomed this legislation, but many feel that it does not go far enough, and that it is not always enforced.

---

1 Do you think it would be easy for Carole to prove that she is being discriminated against? What problems might this cause?
2 What further changes in the law would you like to see?

Women's work

Many people feel that the situation in Britain could be improved. But the plight of women worldwide is much worse, as **B** shows.

A

1857 *Divorce Act* This allowed a man or woman to get a divorce in a court of law rather than by Act of Parliament.
1870 *Married Women's Property Act (1)* Married women could keep their earnings while still living with their husbands.
1875 Women were allowed to go to university.
1882 *Married Women's Property Act (2)* Married women could own property and give it to whoever they wished.
1886 *Guardianship of Infants Act* A mother became the legal parent of her children if the father died.
1886 *Married Women's Act* A husband had to pay his wife maintenance if he deserted her
1918 Women over 30 allowed to vote.
1929 *Equal Franchise Act* Women allowed to vote on the same terms as men.
1949 Women entitled to legal aid in divorce cases
1970 *Equal Pay Act* Women and men to receive the same pay for the same job
1975 *Sex Discrimination Act* It became illegal to discriminate against a person on grounds of sex in education, housing and work
1975 *Employment Protection Act* It became illegal to dismiss a woman because she was pregnant; employers had to pay maternity benefit
1976 *Equal Opportunities Commission* set up to hear complaints about discrimination

---

Women in the developing world may have to combine domestic work, child care and exhausting work on the land. Traditionally, women tend the crops and fetch fuel and water. This often means exhausting work with basic tools, and walking long distances with back-breaking loads.

B

WOMEN
- form 52% of the world's population
- do 65% of the world's work
- work 66% of the world's work hours
- produce 50% of the world's food

YET MEN
- receive 90% of the world's income
- own 99% of the world's property
- make up 90% of government representatives
- earn 25% more than women for doing similar jobs

Gradually, women in the developing world are breaking down these traditional attitudes. Many women play an active role in health programmes and development schemes.

3 Why do you think women are so unfairly treated worldwide?

Housewife's choice?

Until the middle of this century in the UK, it was widely accepted that a woman should give up work when she got married. She would then become a housewife and devote her time to caring for her husband and children.

Over the last 40 years, however, the picture has changed dramatically. Many women have rejected the 'traditional' role of housewife and mother, and demanded the freedom to earn a wage and pursue a career. Some women find themselves torn between being wife/mother and being an independent person. Here is what four women have to say:

C *I would go mad stuck in the house all day. As soon as my baby was old enough to go to a childminder, I went back to work. People tell me I'm missing out on his most precious years, but it's a sacrifice I'm prepared to make.*

D *My husband has always enjoyed working in the house. Now he stays at home and I'm the breadwinner. A lot of men wouldn't be able to cope with that, but it works very well for us.*

E *I get a lot of pressure from my (female) friends, asking me when I'm going back to work. I'm*

almost ashamed to admit that I like being a housewife! I sometimes think the women's movement has gone too far.

F *I think it's important to spend time with my children in the first few years. When they start school, I'll probably go back to work.*

3 Which of these women do you most identify with, and why?
4 Would you be prepared to be a housewife or househusband instead of going out to work?

A matter of opinion

Man for the field and woman for the hearth;
Man for the sword and for the needle she;
Man with the head and woman with the heart;
Man to command and woman to obey;
All else confusion.

Alfred Tennyson

A woman went to buy a new gas cooker. She asked if she could pay over an extended period.

'Certainly, madam,' replied the assistant, 'but I must ask you to get your husband's signature for the hire-purchase agreement.'
'Why?' she asked. 'I have a good job. I can pay my own debts. Why do you need my husband's signature?'
'It's the rule, madam. Your husband is the head of the household so he must sign the agreement.'

Dr Una Kroll *Flesh of my flesh*

- How do you react to each of these extracts? Do you think they show a view of women as second-class citizens?

What does the Bible say?

Ephesians 6, 2

Wives, be subject to your husbands, as to the Lord. For the husband is the head of the wife as Christ is th head of the church ... As the church is subject to Christ, so let wives also be subject in everything to their husbands. Husbands, love your wives, as Christ loved the church and gave himself up for her ... Even so husbands should love their wives as their own bodies. He who loves his wife loves himself.

- What does this passage have to say about women's rights? Do you think it sees women as second-class citizens, or men and women as equal? Explain your answer.

10.1 North and South

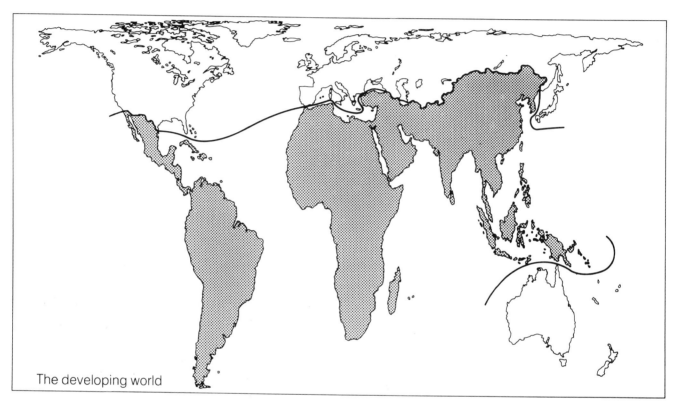

The developing world

A *A divided world – North and South.*

A shows a divided world.

The *North*, or *developed world* (sometimes called the 'first' world) consists of countries with a high standard of living. It includes North America, Western Europe and Australasia.

The *South*, or *developing world* (sometimes called the 'third' world) consists of countries which have a lower standard of living. Some of these countries (eg Sudan, Bangladesh) are very poor; others less so (eg Peru, Colombia, Bolivia).

People also talk about the 'second world'. This refers to Japan and the Communist countries of Eastern Europe, where most people have enough for their needs.

As you can see from map **A**, nearly all the world's poorer countries are south of the dividing line.

Developing countries

About 65–75% of the world's population live in developing countries. These countries have certain features or characteristics in common:

1 Most of the people earn their living from *agriculture*. In the world's poorest countries, 3 out of every 4 men (75% of the population) are involved in agriculture. In Britain the figure is only

6%. Farming in the developing world is largely subsistence farming – that is, people grow just enough to provide for their own needs.

2 Most of the population is *very poor*. A large proportion (possibly the majority) of people are unable to afford the basic necessities of life: enough food, a decent house with sanitation, access to medical care, schools. Many children die before their fifth birthday, from disease or malnutrition. Life expectancy (the age a person can expect to live to) is low. Few people can read or write.

3 The *birth rate* (number of children born for every 1000 of the population) is very high. (You can read more about this in Unit 10.3). Few people reach old age, so a high proportion of the population is under 15.

---

1 Find out all you can about one developing country. Imagine what it would be like to be a young person there. Draw up a chart comparing their life with yours, for example:

UK	Developing country
Semi-detached house	Sleeps on pavement
3 meals a day	1 bowl of rice and vegetables

The Brandt Report

In 1980 a group of political and economic experts drew up the *Brandt Report*. This focused attention on the wide gap between the rich and poor countries of the world. The Report revealed that the developed countries of the North have a quarter of the world's population and four-fifths of its income. The developing countries of the South have three-quarters of the world's population, but only one fifth of its income.

The Brandt Report painted a bleak picture of life in the developing world (**B**).

B *Many hundreds of millions of people in the poorer countries are preoccupied solely with survival and elementary needs. For them work is frequently not available or, when it is, pay is very low and conditions often barely tolerable. Homes are constructed of impermeable (non-waterproof)* materials and have neither piped water nor sanitation. Electricity is a luxury ... Primary schools, where they exist, may be free and not too far away, but children are needed for work and cannot easily be spared for schooling ... Flood, drought or disease affecting people or livestock can destroy livelihoods without hope of compensation.

---

2 Rewrite the first sentence of this extract in your own words.
3 Try to find out what is being done to help solve some of these problems (eg work of United Nations relief agencies; organisations like Oxfam, Cafod, Muslim Aid ...). Write a report of your findings.

One world?

The *Brandt Report* pointed out that despite the divide between North and South, all the world's countries are *interdependent*. We all live on one planet – what happens in one part of the world can affect people thousands of miles away. The rich countries of the world have a duty to help the poorer countries – and it is in their own interest to do so.

---

4 Do you agree that the rich countries of the world have a duty to help the poorer countries? Or do you think that the countries of the South should solve their own problems? Explain your answer.
5 What do you understand by the idea of 'one world' and 'interdependence'? Can you think of any examples of how countries depend on each other?

What does the Bible say?

Mark 10. 23–28
Jesus looked around and said to his disciples, 'How hard it will be for those who have riches to enter the kingdom of God!' And the disciples were amazed at his words. But Jesus said to them again, 'Children, how hard it is to enter the kingdom of God! It is easier for a camel to go through the eye of a needle than for a rich man to enter the kingdom of God.'

● What does this suggest about the Christian attitude to world poverty?

10.2 Natural disasters

Every time you turn on the news there has been another disaster. Floods in one place, famine in another, typhoons, earthquakes ... If there is a God, how can he let these things happen?

Ian, 16

Christians and non-Christians have been asking this question for centuries, and are still no closer to an answer. Every year, terrible disasters hit the headlines and we read accounts of millions of people suffering.

Acts of God?

Natural disasters are sometimes described as 'acts of God'. Why?

1 In ancient times, people believed that spirits or gods lived in the earth, sea and sky. Disasters were caused by evil spirits, or by wars between the gods. People offered gifts and sacrifices to try to please the gods and avert disasters.
2 Modern science gives us the answer to many of life's mysteries. But natural disasters still seem to come 'out of the blue'. Some people think of them as 'chance' occurrences. Others say they are 'the will of God'.
3 Natural disasters are completely beyond human control. People cannot protect themselves. Disasters remind us all that we are frail human beings.

---

1 Do you think that calling a disaster an 'Act of God' helps people come to terms with it? Or is it a way of avoiding the issue and not doing anything about the problem?

Disaster strikes

Another disaster strikes in the third world (**A**). Thousands of people die. Thousands more are made homeless.

Developing countries do not have the resources or the technology to launch effective rescue operations when disaster strikes. It may take days for people to reach the affected area. International organisations such as Oxfam, the Red Cross and Christian Aid play a vital part in mounting disaster appeals and getting emergency supplies to those in need. But responding to disasters is only a small part of the work of these organisations, as you can see in Units 10.3–10.5

---

2 How do you feel when you are asked to contribute to a disaster fund? Relieved that you are safe? Sorry for the victims? Guilty that you aren't doing more to help? What elements make up a successful appeal?

How can God let this happen?

This is one of the hardest questions to answer. Christians say that they worship a God of love. Yet if God is loving and all-powerful, how does he allow these disasters to take place?

According to the Bible, God created a perfect world.

B Genesis 1.31
And God saw everything that he had made, and behold, it was very good.

Most Christians accept that the creation story is not meant to be taken literally. A few, however, believe that it is a true account. They argue that human sin and evil are responsible for the suffering in the world. Natural disasters are caused by forces of evil, or the Devil. Clearly, some disasters may be partially caused by human interference with the natural environment, but this cannot account for most tragedies.

In the Old Testament, natural disasters such as plagues or famine are often presented as punishments sent by God. In the Book of Exodus, for

A *When natural disasters strike in the developing world, thousands lose their homes and all their possessions.*

example, God sends seven 'plagues' on the Egyptians, until they let Moses and his followers go.

C Exodus 9.23–25
... and the Lord sent thunder and hail, and fire ran down to the earth. And the Lord rained hail upon the land of Egypt; there was hail, and fire flashing continually in the midst of the hail, very heavy hail, such as had never been in all the land of Egypt since it became a nation. The hail struck down everything that was in the field throughout all the land of Egypt, both man and beast; and the hail struck down every plant of the field, and shattered every tree of the field.

Few people today, however, see natural disasters as a judgement from God. Moreover, the victims are often some of the poorest people in the world, who could not be considered as 'sinners'.

Clearly, neither of these is an adequate answer. Christians simply cannot explain the dilemma. All they can do in the face of such suffering is trust God and believe that he, too, is involved in the pain. This is not to say that Christians should passively accept all the tragedy in the world. Rather, their religious beliefs prompt them to devote time, resources and effort to help the suffering at home and abroad.

---

3 Do natural disasters make it difficult – or impossible – to believe in a loving God?
4 Can you see any way in which good might come out of a natural disaster?

10.3 Too many people?

When we got married, my husband and I decided we would have two children. We can't afford a big family, and I wanted to get back to my career as quickly as I could.

Moira, 34, UK solicitor

I have five children – two daughters and three sons. We had two more, but they died when they were babies. The girls help my wife in the house and my sons work on the land with me. Even the youngest (he's 6) helps gather wood and scare the birds. Our children will look after us when we are old. We couldn't manage without them.

Paolo, smallholder, Colombia

By the time you have read to the bottom of this page, 50 babies will have been born!

Every second, somewhere in the world, four babies are born. World population is growing by 2% every year. Experts predict that by the year 2000, the population will have shot up to somewhere between 6,000,000,000 and 8,000,000,000 (see **A**). This dramatic increase is sometimes known as the 'population explosion'.

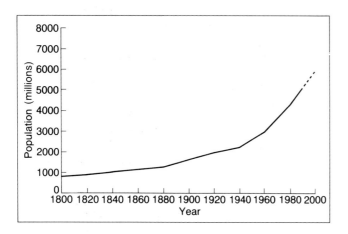

A *The 'population explosion'.*

---

1 Do you find these figures surprising? Alarming? What problems do you think the population explosion might cause in the future?

The population is not increasing at the same rate everywhere. Moira and her husband are typical of people in the developed world; they have decided to limit their family to two children. In some developed countries, the population growth has slowed down altogether. Norway, Sweden and Switzerland are concerned that their population is actually declining. This means that there will be a higher proportion of old people – and fewer people of working age.

In many developing countries population growth is much faster. In Kenya, for example, the population is increasing by about 8% each year. By the year 2000 it seems likely that 1 in every 4 people will be Chinese (**B**).

Why do people in the developing world have more children? Paolo gave some of the answers. **C** shows factors that influence family size in the developed and developing worlds.

City life

As we saw in Unit 10.1, many people in the developing world rely on what they can grow or produce for survival. As the population increases, it becomes more and more difficult to scrape a living on the land. Many people move to cities to try and find work – some end up living in slums, shanty towns, or even on the streets.

About 50% of the world's population now live in cities. Mexico City is the world's largest city, with a population of 14.8 million.

Can population growth be slowed down?

Many governments in the developing world are alarmed at the rapid population growth in their countries, and have taken measures to try to slow it down.

B *As populations continue to grow, the pressure on the world's cities and resources increases.*

In India, for example, there was a mass sterilisation and contraception campaign. Men were rewarded with a cow if they volunteered for sterilisation. Women received a radio if they had a contraceptive device fitted. The campaign lasted for five years, but it was not a success. Only 1,000,000 men came forward for sterilisation.

In China, the government has imposed a strict 'one child' policy. Most second pregnancies are aborted. If a couple do go on to have a second child, they face heavy taxes and other financial penalties. Despite this campaign, however, the Chinese population continues to grow rapidly.

Countries with a largely Roman Catholic population face particular difficulties, since the Roman Catholic Church is opposed to any 'unnatural' form of birth control (see Unit 2.8).

C

In the developing world:	In the developed world:
• Children do domestic chores like collecting fuel and water • Children look after the animals and help on the land • Children may earn money for food, clothing etc. • Children care for younger brothers and sisters • Children look after parents when they are old.	• Children need expensive clothing, toys, equipment • Most children stay at school until they are 16 – extra lessons, equipment etc have to be paid for • Larger families may mean larger, more expensive houses etc.

2 Can you suggest why the Indian birth control campaign was not a success?
3 Do you think it is right:
  a) For a government to try to bribe people to have fewer children?
  b) For a government to force people to limit their families?
  Give reasons for your answers.
4 Can you think of any alternative solution to the population explosion in the developing world?

A matter of opinion

No wonder people in the developing world have problems – they all have too many children. If you ask me, compulsory sterilisation is the only answer.

• Do you think compulsory birth control can ever be justified?
• Do you think population growth is the only cause of problems in the developing world (look back at Unit 10.1 to help you)?

10.4 World hunger

They say there's enough food in the world to feed everyone. Yet there are all these famines and appeals for aid for starving people in the Third World. It seems ridiculous that we have so much and they have nothing. Why can't we send our grain mountains and wine lakes to the people who really need them?

Asif, 16

A lot of people ask this question, and it is difficult to find a satisfactory answer. The problem of world hunger is less to do with food supplies than with politics, economics and power.

A   Hunger – the facts

Hunger and related diseases kills more people than war. Malnutrition kills . . .
1 person every 2.5 seconds
24 people every minute
35,000 people every day
20,000,000 people every year.
75% of those who die are children under 5.

Understanding world hunger

World hunger is a complicated problem, which is often misunderstood.

Misunderstanding 1: *There is not enough food to go round.* The simple truth is that there is plenty of food in the world – enough to feed all the world's starving people (**B**).

Each year vast amounts of that food are simply destroyed. The main problem is that most of the food is in the wrong place – in the developed world. For example, the US, with only 6% of the world's population, consumes (and wastes) 35% of the world's food.

B   The answer to world hunger?

- There are 3500 calories per kilo of grain so a ton of grain supplies an average of 3,500,000 calories.
- The Food and Agricultural Organisation says that about 2300 calories a day is usually adequate for proper nutrition.
- At 2300 calories a day for 365 days each person would need 839,500 calories a year which means that each ton of grain could provide for over four people.
- A million tons would feed more than 4,000,000 people. To cover all the people who now die from malnutrition each year would take just five million tons of grain altogether.

Susan George, *quoted* on *The Politics of Food* Channel 4 TV

---

1 Look at **B**. Can you see any flaws in the argument?
2 If governments in the developed world decided to give their food surpluses to developing countries, what practical problems might arise? Can you suggest how these might be solved?

Misunderstanding 2: *World hunger is caused by over-population*

It is true that the population of many countries is increasing very rapidly (see Unit 10.2). It is also true that the fastest increase tends to be in countries which have a severe food problem.

However, in terms of population density (number of people per square kilometre) the picture looks rather different. There are an average 98 people per square kilometre in Western Europe. In Africa, the figure is just 18 per square kilometre. The problem is that in many poorer countries the land is infertile (eg desert or mountain) and people cannot afford the technology to improve it. So overcrowded Western Europe is ale to feed all its people, while in sparsely-populated Africa millions starve.

Misunderstanding 3: *Starvation is the result of drought, floods and earthquakes*

Natural disasters do not only hit the developing world. Developed countries have their share of catastrophes. For example, there was a serious drought in the mid-West of the United States in 1988. But no-one died. A similar disaster in a developing country such as Sudan would result in famine and starvation for millions.

Why the difference? The rich US has mountains of stored grain and the transport to distribute it. It can also offer financial and technical aid to the farmers, to help them get back on their feet. Developing countries have no stored grain and little available transport. People are forced to eat their seed corn, so there may be no harvest for many years to come.

Misunderstanding 4: *Science can cure world hunger*

In the 1960s and 70s scientists worked hard to develop new, higher-yielding strains of wheat and rice. During the so-called 'Green Revolution' these were introduced into some developing countries. They brought some improvements, but not the miraculous results hoped for.

By way of definition

Malnutrition is a lack of essential nutrients. Someone may suffer from malnutrition if they do not have enough food, or if they do not have a well-balanced diet. The problem is often made worse by diarrhoea and dysentery.

The Green Revolution was an attempt by scientists to produce new strains of grain which would grow well in harsh conditions.

Who helps?

Many national and international agencies exist to provide aid to the developing world. Among the most famous are Oxfam, War on Want and Save the Children Fund. There are also religious organisations such as Christian Aid, Cafod and Muslim Aid. Relief agancies aim to provide:

- short-term crisis or 'disaster' aid, such as food or urgently-needed medical supplies after a natural disaster (C);
- small-scale appropriate aid, such as farming equipment, to help local people set up their own improvement schemes;
- long-term aid, such as health projects and education schemes, which aim to ensure a better future.

Many governments also provide loans to developing countries, for such things as major irrigation schemes or road construction.

---

3 Find out as much as you can about the work of *one* relief agency.

C *Relief agencies like Oxfam supply short-term food aid when there is a crisis. But this is only a small part of their work. The problem of world hunger can only be solved by long-term planning.*

What does the Bible say?

Luke 6. 20–25
And (Jesus) lifted up his eyes on his disciples, and said:
'Blessed are you poor, for yours is the kingdom of God.
Blessed are you that hunger now, for you shall be satisfied.
Blessed are you that weep now, for you shall laugh.
. . . .
But woe to you that are rich, for you have received your consolation.
Woe to you that are full now, for you shall hunger.
Woe to you that laugh now, for you shall mourn and weep . . .

- How would you interpret these words?

A matter of opinion

I asked the men, 'What are you carrying wrapped in that hammock, brothers?'
And they answered, 'We carry a dead body, brother.'
So I asked, 'Was he killed or did he die a natural death?'
'That is difficult to answer, brother. It seems more to have been a murder.'
'How was the man killed?' I asked. 'With a knife or a bullet, brothers?'
'It was neither a knife nor a bullet; it was a much more perfect crime. One that leaves no sign.'
'Then how did they kill this man?' I asked.
They calmly answered: 'This man was killed by hunger, brother?'

- Was it murder? If so, who was the murderer?

10.5 Education and literacy

I've always taken education for granted. I often moan about school being boring and a waste of time. But recently we had a visiting student from Nigeria. He told us what a privilege it was to be able to go to school. He used to walk 5 miles a day, and the school had hardly any books or equipment. I'd never thought about it like that before.

Simon, 15

Think for a moment about what it would be like if you were unable to read or write. Of course, you wouldn't be able to read this book. Nor would you be able to browse through a newspaper or magazine, fill in forms, read street names . . . Later on, you might find it difficult to get a job, or even to vote in an election.

About 1% of the UK population is **illiterate** (unable to read or write). In many developing countries, however, people receive little or no education and the majority of the population is illiterate. **A** shows literacy figures for 20 countries.

Education and wealth

From chart **A** you can see that most of the countries with a high literacy rate are in the North or developed world. It is no coincidence that these are also the world's wealthiest countries.

---

1 Why do you think there is such a close link between education and wealth?

Countries with more than 50% illiteracy are very often the world's poorest countries, where the fight for survival uses up all available finance and resources. Faced with hunger, poverty, war, poor communications and failing crops, it is hardly surprising that governments do not make education a high priority. After all, people do not die for lack of education!

Country	% literacy
Australia	99
Bangladesh	29
Burkina Faso	9
Canada	96
China	65
Cuba	98
East Germany	100
Ethiopia	62
France	99
India	65
Japan	100
Niger	10
Nigeria	34
Papua New Guinea	32
Saudi Arabia	25
Sudan	31
UK	99
USA	99
USSR	100
West Germany	100

A *Levels of literacy in 20 countries.*

Most poor countries are locked into a 'vicious cycle' when it comes to education (**B**).

---

2 How does illiteracy increase a poor country's problems?
3 Should the governments of developing countries spend more on education? (Remember, this may mean cutting down on urgent short-term needs.)

What is being done to help?

The United Nations Educational, Scientific and Cultural Organisation (UNESCO) leads international efforts to help poor countries improve their education services. UNESCO depends on aid provided by richer countries, like Britain. Yet the amount Britain provides has decreased.

Another possibility is for poorer countries to send people to developed countries to train as teachers, nurses and doctors. In the past, Britain welcomed a large number of overseas students. But recently the Government decided to increase the fees paid by foreign students in colleges and universities and the number has gone down.

Several countries have done a great deal to help themselves C. For example, Nicaragua and Cuba launched very successful 'literacy drives'. Children and young people are educated to a certain level, and then sent out to teach those who are still illiterate. Often they start with other members of their own families. In Cuba, this has raised the literacy level to 98%.

Only 25% of the population between 11 and 15 go to school.

So few people receive schooling after the age of 11

Few of these go on to further education

This leads to a shortage of teachers to train

B *The vicious cycle of illiteracy.*

C *Outdoor schools like this can help raise the literacy rate in developing countries.*

---

4 Do you think that richer countries have a responsibility to help poor countries provide education, or should developing countries help themselves? Explain your answer.

A matter of opinion

The measure of whether a country cares about its own people is the extent to which it is not only concerned to put food in its people's mouths, but also to build schools so that its people can receive an elementary education. Without such an education its people can do little to stave off the starvation which will inevitably come.

● Explain in your own words why literacy is important.

10.6 Nuclear power

When they decided to build a nuclear power station near here there was a public outcry. We had meetings and protest marches and even sent a petition to Parliament. The local MP came and explained all the advantages: employment for local people, a cheap source of energy. He said nuclear reactors are perfectly safe, but I'm not so sure.

Angela, 17

Would you feel like Angela if there were plans to build a nuclear reactor near you? Most people feel uneasy about nuclear power. The accident at Chernobyl in 1986 made people very aware of the potential risks involved.

Do we need nuclear power?

8% of the world's electricity is now generated by nuclear power. In the USA, Belgium, Sweden and West Germany the figure is much higher. Britain gets almost 20% of its electricity from nuclear power stations, and there are plans to build more.

Supporters of nuclear power argue that:

- the world's oil deposits are running out. Nuclear power is the best alternative to oil-fired power stations.
- a nuclear power station only uses small amounts of fuel. The new 'breeder' reactors can create their own fuel. All that is needed is a plentiful supply of water for cooling. Nuclear power preserves the earth's resources.
- although nuclear power stations are expensive to build, running costs are low.

Opponents of nuclear power argue that:

- nuclear reactors use uranium and plutonium. These are both radioactive. Increased radioactivity in the atmosphere causes cancer, leukaemia and deformities in unborn babies.
- radioactive waste cannot be destroyed. It has to be dumped somewhere, and remains dangerous for thousands of years. Transporting the waste is also risky.

- accidents can, and do, happen at nuclear power stations. There have been small leakages of radioactive material from the power station at Sellafield in Cumbria. It is not yet known how many people were affected by the fire at Chernobyl in 1986.
- the plutonium used for power stations can also be used to make nuclear weapons.

---

1 Look at the arguments for and against nuclear power. Which do you think are the most persuasive, and why?

Alternatives to nuclear power

Opponents of nuclear power argue that it is not the only alternative to fuels such as oil and coal, which are now running out. They maintain that alternative sources of energy, such as wind power and solar power, should be developed. These are cheap to run, they do not use up the earth's resources, and do not have dangerous side-effects. You can read more about alternative energy in Unit 10.8.

---

2 Do you think more time and money should be spent on investigating alternative forms of energy? Why?

A matter of opinion

Nuclear power is one of God's greatest gifts to the human race. Used properly it could solve many of mankind's most worrying problems.

We've got the technology. It would be a stupid waste not to use it. Far better to develop nuclear generators than nuclear weapons anyway.

The risks are simply too high. It's all very well scientists and politicians assuring us that nuclear reactors are safe. You don't see many of them living next to one, do you?

- Which (if any) of these viewpoints do you agree with, and why?

10.7 Pollution

We were on holiday in Germany recently and we came across miles and miles of dead trees. When we asked a local man what had killed them he said 'acid rain'. My Dad told me that this is caused by a build-up of chemicals in the air. But the worst thing is that Britain produces a lot more air pollution than some other countries. We're responsible for killing German trees! Why doesn't the government do something?

Jason, 14

Acid rain is caused by a build-up of sulphur dioxide and nitrogen in the atmosphere. The wind carries this polluted air to Germany and Scandinavia, where the pollution can destroy life in lakes and forests, and erode stonework and buildings.

Pollution can also happen overnight, with disastrous consequences. A huge spillage of oil off Alaska in 1989 produced an oil slick the size of the UK and killed fish and seabirds in the region.

A   *A victim of oil pollution.*

Different kinds of pollution

Earth, air and water are essential to life. Yet humankind does terrible – often irreparable – damage to the environment.

1 *Polluting the sea*   Around 70% of the earth's surface is covered by water. In recent years, vast areas of coastline have been polluted by sewage and industrial waste. According to a recent report, it is only safe to swim in the sea off 25% of Britain's beaches. The Mediterranean Sea is also heavily polluted.

2 *Polluting the air*   Most cities in Britain are designated as 'clean air zones', which means that there are restrictions on smoke and fumes. The old 'pea-souper' smogs may have gone, but a thick layer of chemicals blankets many of the world's industrial cities, such as San Francisco in the US.

The earth is surrounded by a protective 'ozone layer' which filters out the dangerous ultra-violet rays of the sun. Scientists have discovered holes in this layer – caused by, among other things, the exhausts of high-flying aircraft, and aerosol sprays.

3 *Polluting the earth*   The chemicals farmers use to increase crop yields and produce more food may in fact poison the earth for future generations. Chemical fertilisers build up in the earth and wash into streams and rivers, poisoning fish and wildlife. Pesticides sprayed over crops kill all insects – not just the pest they are designed to eradicate. Environmentalists are concerned about the effects this will have on other creatures – and ultimately on humankind.

Accidental chemical leaks can also have horrific consequences. At least 2000 people were killed by a chemical leak at Bhopal in India in 1984; many more were blinded or suffered long-term effects. A fire at a chemical factory in Basle, Switzerland, in 1986 polluted the Rhine and wiped out its fish stocks.

1 Which forms of pollution do you find particularly worrying and why?
2 Do you think the British government does enough to prevent pollution?
3 Do we have a responsibility to think of future generations and make sure that we leave them a living planet?

How can we help?

Faced with such a grim picture, it is easy to feel helpless. But there are things that individuals can do to help preserve the environment. You can read more about them in the next unit.

10.8 Conservation – who cares?

The last units have painted a very bleak picture of the future: increasing population, dwindling natural resources, pollution and destruction on a massive scale. Many people are deeply concerned about the future of the planet, and are taking positive action to protect and conserve the environment.

What can we do? A shows some of the ideas one class suggested:

Bottle bank

use recycled loo paper

SOLAR POWER

BICYCLES

Save newspaper, aluminium foil, tin cans for Friends of the Earth

become vegetarian

use 'environmentally friendly products'

Grow organic foods

Never throw away litter

Sometimes it is hard to see what difference we can make. Surely the answer lies with government action: Big business? Industrialists?

B *It is easy to say that it is up to Governments and industry to put things right but, in practice, it is what we do and what we buy or reject that dictates what industry or Governments do. We are all, in some small way, responsible for what happens to the world as a whole. We can no longer ignore the fact that if each of us in our everyday life does not do something about it, we may soon not have a world fit to live in.*

(from *Doing our bit – A practical guide to the environment and what we can do about it* Hugh and Margaret Brown)

---

1 Study **A**. Can you think of any other ideas?
2 Do you agree with the authors of **B**, that we are *all* responsible for what happens to the world? Explain your reasons.
3 Find out about conservation groups near you. For example, is there a local branch of Friends of the Earth; does your district have a Green Party representative? Invite a representative to come and talk to your class or group.
4 Follow up one of these ideas in your class – or the school.

Conserve or develop?

Conservation is not a clear-cut issue – with developers and industrialists as the 'baddies' and environmentalists as the 'goodies'. Many factors need to be considered. For example, we may protest about houses being built on green fields – but people need somewhere to live.

The issues are even more complex for many developing countries, which may feel they cannot afford the 'luxury' of preserving the environment in their struggle for development. However, developing countries are making efforts to preserve the environment, as the following examples show:

1 The greening of China

The Chinese government has launched a massive tree-planting scheme. They aim to achieve 30% tree cover over the entire country. Workers have 'holidays' planting trees on wasteland, roadsides and railways. 'Honeymoon' plantations encourage newly-weds to plant a tree. If a group fails to meet its target for tree-planting, or if anyone fells a tree illegally, they face heavy fines.

2 Community forestry in Nepal

Deforestation (felling of trees) is a serious problem in Nepal. Experts predict that the country's forests could be destroyed in 15 years. The Government has set up a major community forestry effort to save the trees. Local people are encouraged to plant trees and save energy. So far, 250,000 trees have been planted; dams, canals and terraces have been built or renovated and 15,000 energy-saving domestic stoves have been introduced.

---

5 Find out as much as you can about the problem of **deforestation** (tree felling on a massive scale) and its effects. How are China and Nepal trying to solve this problem?

A Christian responsibility?

Many Christians feel that they have a particular duty to care for the environment. They believe that God created the world for people to enjoy – it is up to us to care for the world and not destroy it.

C Genesis 1.26–28
Then God said, 'Let us make man in our image, after our likeness; and let them have dominion over the fish of the sea, and over the birds of the air, and over the cattle, and over all the earth, and over every creeping thing that creeps upon the earth.' So God created man in his own image, in the image of God he created him; male and female he created them. And God blessed them, and God said to them, 'Be fruitful and multiply, and fill the earth and subdue it; and have dominion over the fish of the sea and over the birds of the air and over every living thing that moves upon the earth.'

---

6 What do you understand by the words 'subdue' and 'have dominion over'?
7 Are Christians right to feel they have a special responsibility to care for the planet?

10.9 Greenpeace

A *Greenpeace volunteers are doing a lot of dirty work for the rest of us. How else would we have known about the slaughter of whales or seal cubs? How else could we have appreciated the dangers of ocean pollution, the extraordinary risks that are being taken with nuclear waste?*

The politicians will not freely tell us of what is happening to the environment. The vested interests of large corporations will not come clean unless we force them. That is why Greenpeace have had to take the moral initiative – always non-violently, always carefully.

Extract **A** comes from a publicity leaflet for Greenpeace, the international environmental pressure group. Peaceful direct action by Greenpeace has encouraged people to demand changes in the law.

What does Greenpeace stand for?

- a safe and nuclear-free world
- fresh air
- clean water
- the protection of wildlife and its habitat

Successes

In the last few years, Greenpeace volunteers have:

1 Sailed into a French nuclear test zone – Amchitka in the Aleutian Islands. The French no longer test nuclear weapons in the atmosphere. This test zone is now a bird sanctuary.
2 Sailed tiny inflatable dinghies between harpoons and whales. The slaughter of whales has been reduced to a fraction of the 42,000 being killed a decade ago.
3 Prevented the slaughter of 200,000 baby seals a year and suppressed the trade in seal pelts.
4 Fought a long and successful campaign against dumping radioactive waste into the Irish sea.
5 Campaigned successfully against the burning of hazardous chemical waste in the North Sea, the waters around the US and the Mediterrnean.

1 Why do you think action by Greenpeace has been so successful?
2 Find out as much as you can about current Greenpeace campaigns.

A matter of opinion

PLANET EARTH IS 4600 MILLION YEAR OLD

If we condense this inconceivable time-span into an understandable concept, we can liken Earth to a person of 46 years of age.

Nothing is known of the first 7 years of this person's life, and whilst only scattered information exists about the middle span, we know that at only age 42 did the Earth begin to flower. Dinosaurs and the great reptiles did not appear until one year ago when the planet was 45. Mammals arrived only eight months ago; in the middle of last week man-like apes evolved into ape-like men, and at the weekend the last ice age enveloped earth. Modern man has been round for 4 hours. During the last hour Man discovered agriculture. The industrial revolution began a minute ago.

During those sixty seconds of biological time Modern man has made a rubbish tip of Paradise.

He has multiplied his numbers to plague proportions, caused the extinction of 500 species of animals, ransacked the planet for fuels and now stands like a brutish infant, gloating over this meteoric rise to ascendancy, on the brink of a war to end all wars and of effectively destroying this oasis of life in the solar system.

- What is your reaction to this article?